letters to her.

Dalton Hessel

letters to her. copyright © 2018 Dalton Hessel

All rights reserved.

ISBN: 1720847517

ISBN-13: 978-1720847519

All rights reserved. Printed in the United States. No part of this book may be used or reproduced in any manner whatsoever without written permission except in the case of reprints in the context of reviews.

Printed in the United States of America

First Printing: November 2018

Dalton Hessel

P.O. Box 1264

Hayward, WI 54843

Facebook: Dalton Hessel's Writings

Instagram: @hessel_themanintheballcap

#letterstoher #daltonhesselwritings

Author Illustrations created by David Ardinaryas Lojaya

to the hopeful romantics.

SEASONS

	acknowledgments	i
1	author's note	3
2	fall.	pg #4
3	winter.	pg #56
4	spring.	pg #120
5	summer.	pg #185

ACKNOWLEDGMENTS

Thank you to the people that have told me not to give up on an extraordinary love. Thank you to those who have modeled to me what love looks like. Thank you to my sister Allison for nights out on the front porch talking about love and relationships. Your insight and wisdom is something that I truly value and I don't know what I would do without our conversations. Thank you to Mike Hansen for the bike rides to get my mind off of things for a while. Thank you to Dick Robbins for the conversations at the coffee shop about life and seeing silver linings. Thank you to Sonofmel and Farmstead Creamery and Café for hosting Spoken Word sessions on Thursday nights. Those summer nights provided me with an opportunity to share my words with an audience for the first time. Thank you to Ashley, Ian, Matt, and Linsey of The Whistle Punk for your continued support. I love you guys. Thank you to Backroads Coffee for giving me a second home to write in. Thank you to my editors: Megan Ellison, Lucy Horst and Natalie Hegna. Thank you for continually humbling me. There's something comforting in the notes you write next to all of the edits you made. I owe you all a great meal at Dooley's. Thank you to those that follow me on social media and have left words of encouragement. You have no idea what those little comments do for me on the days when coffee no longer seems to motivate me and my pencil rests on a blank sheet of notebook paper. Finally, thank you to her. Thank you for giving me hope about the past, present and future. I'm going to give you all I've got as we write our story together.

AUHTOR'S NOTE

"To every thing there is a season, and a time to do every purpose under heaven…"

Ecclesiastes 3:1

There's a season for every time in our lives. We will find ourselves in seasons of singleness and in seasons of love. The seasons of singleness can feel as though they are more brutal than any winter that we have yet to experience. We zip up our jackets to hide from the wind and our friends that are in relationships or are married. We wonder why we can't have what they have. Your season of singleness will eventually end. "Be patient," is what people will tell you. That's easier said than done. Sometimes it will feel like you're wasting your breath, but I promise you that's when your faith is most prevalent. You'll find that person and when you do, it'll all make sense. All of the waiting, praying, and working on yourself.

"Marriage is only as good as your singleness. If you don't work on your singleness, you'll be frustrated in your marriage. Singleness may be the most important time of your life." – Pastor Michael Todd

These letters to her are my form of working on my singleness. With each letter that I write to her, it's my form of a prayer. They aren't all love letters for sometimes I grow frustrated with love. My hope with every letter is that I'm working on changing seasons.

FALL.

love is a verb.

you can talk until
your face turns red and the veins in your neck stick out.
you can send emojis and sweet texts until your phone dies.
you can sing about it in your car
or watch movies about it in a dark room with strangers.
but if you were taught correctly
you'd know that a verb is an action.

love as a verb means
lending her your jacket, even when it's cold outside.
it means hugging her and letting her sob
into your chest when her world seems to be
crashing down.

it means eating the meal she cooked and not leaving
anything on your plate no matter how burnt
or undercooked it was.
it means reading practice quiz questions to her
instead of watching the game night.
it means all of these things and so much more.

love is a verb, so start taking action.

too good.

you look too good in my sweatshirt.
the one with the frayed edges that graces your body
so often on friday nights when we are feeling anti-social.
you look too good in my hat.
the brewers one that has paint splattered all over it
from that time we tried
being chip and jo in our living room.
don't think i have forgotten about
that "accidental" dropping of the paintbrush.
i don't think i'll ever let you live that one down.

you look too good across from me at the dinner table.
grace flows out of your mouth like a river before we dive
into another breakfast-for-dinner night.
i soak up our conversations, our laughter, and your beauty
more than the stack of buttermilk pancakes that sit before
me, awaiting the arrival of their maple syrup companion.

you look too good in the seat next to me.
you're next to me at the theater on $5 tuesdays
toting your free bag of popcorn and a large sprite.

you're next to me in the bleachers in your chucks
and a game face on.
you're next to me in the car fiddling with the aux
and playing my guilty pleasures.
i try to limit you to one snapchat video of us,
but it is no use.

you're next to me in the photos of us together
with our smiles as wide as we can get them.

"you're too good for me"
is what they keep telling me and I believe them.

but I am glad I said, "hello,"
on the day nobody else had the courage to.

because that'd be crazy.

every thought that i have about you is overanalyzed.
what i am going to say to you has to be well thought out.
i fear that if i say or do the wrong thing
you'll run away and never come back.

we're supposed to love without fear.
we're not supposed to have to worry
or doubt in our hearts.
if this is the case the case, why do i hesitate before i
hit the send button on every text message?

i want to be the type of man that chases you every day,
but i don't want to smother you.

why can't i throw rocks at your window?
why can't i sweep you off of your feet at work
and take you on a spontaneous road trip?
it's because the fear is still there,
lingering like a dog waiting to be let in from the cold.
so, i don't do any of those crazy things.
i just play it safe and say, "hope you had a good day."

changes.

everybody has a heartbreak that changed them.
everybody can tell you the name of the person
that temporarily broke them.
they can tell you what they were wearing,
what the weather was like that day or night,
who they called right after it happened,
what items were thrown out first,
what items were thrown out last,
and what items they decided to hold onto.

they don't say these things out loud anymore,
but they hold on to these tiny nuggets
of information about that person.

they can't help it.

they remember the little things like what they normally
ordered at subway to the way their fragrance smells like
in the backseat of a chevy.
just because someone breaks our hearts,
it doesn't mean we will be forever broken.
we heal in our own ways.

when heartbreak happens, we wish the rest of the world
would pause and collectively grieve with us.
we wish that the cashier knew what
we were going through.
we wish that our bosses wouldn't be as tough
on deadlines this week.
we wish that the pizza delivery guy would just accept the
damn money slid to him from under the door
and leave the pizza outside.
the radio in our cars isn't broken
but driving in silence is better than
risking hearing that song.

everybody has a heartbreak that has changed them,
but they don't remain heartbroken forever.
no, they end up rebuilding eventually,
but they're a little slower to open doors.
car doors. front doors. restaurant doors.
all of these doors they used to open for other people have
left them in a state of homelessness.

they'll find their home eventually
and won't shiver every time there's a knock.

my files.

with a little half and half:
that's the way she likes her coffee.
with a surprise hug and lips brought to her forehead:
that's the way she likes her kisses.
with melting raisinets thrown in:
that's the way she likes her popcorn at the movies.
with the knob turned about ¾ of the way:
that's the way she likes her baths to be run.
with a good book:
that's the way she gets ready for bed.

the right side of her body is the most ticklish.
the best way to get her to smile is to make
a face like you just got electrocuted.

the best way to comfort her is to
sit down beside her
listen to her
and tell her everything is going to be alright.

how do i know this?

she didn't tell me upfront.

it's the mental images and documents

i've been storing away for a while now.

every day, old information helps me comprehend the new.

i learn something different about her with each

sunrise and each sunset.

i pray my hard drive is never erased.

trail runner.

the best advice i was ever given was,
"be sure to chase her every day."
it doesn't always have to be big things because God knows
i don't have the money to be sending
maroon 5 to sing to her at work.
it's being intentional with your actions.

picking up after yourself
without having to be asked.
making her favorite meal.
leaving notes on the counter for her.
helping her out if she's running late.
going to events that you don't care for but being
present for her.

if it's a burden for you to chase her
don't fall for that woman.
don't waste your time,
don't waste her time.

pulling the pin.

carefully thought out insults can feel like
an airstrike on your heart.
there are other times when we fire off
our mouths like machine guns,
not caring what we destroy in the process.
there are moments of peace when all seems well,
but then you look back at
the destruction, and know that
it will be difficult to rebuild.

do you rebuild where you once battled
or do you move on to another potential war zone?

every little thing is going to be alright.

i hate to see you sad.
it's not the holy-crap-i-think-she's-going-to-dehydrate-
herself-from-all-of-her-crying sob that gets to me.
it's the look in your eyes.
i hate it when you doubt yourself and what you can do.
i want to give you the most inspirational speech
to let you know that you can do it,
but it ultimately comes down to you.

you're smart
you're confident when you want to be
and you say all of the things that i am too shy to utter.
when the weight of the world seems to press down
on your shoulders

just breathe.

i'm not going to tell you to calm down
i'm not going to pretend like stress
isn't going to come up in our lives,
but when it all seems to be too much,
i want you to know that i am here
to help ease the burden in any way i can.

focus.

my focus is something that you always have.
you have it when the faces of those in the restaurant
could easily conceal yours.
i look past the kids squirming in their seats
as they refuse to eat despite the airplane
trying to fly into their mouths.

i look past the men telling tall tales from out on the water
and the fish they never caught.
i look past the group of women sipping on martinis
and talking about a book only a few of them actually read.

all i see is you.

i focus on you when you wave at the little children
in car seats that we pass along the highway.
i focus on you when you're reading on the front porch
during a thunderstorm.
the flashes of lightning illuminate your face
as your eyes dart down the pages.
the wind turns your pages as it tries to force you
to be a speed reader.

you bite your lip and conjure up your own method of
holding back the pages.

i focus on you when we cook together.
you love a little chaos in the kitchen
and aren't afraid to make a little mess,
even though i'm the constant byproduct of your
shenanigans.

i focus on you during the sad parts of the movies.
i extend my hand out to you as an offering
and you squeeze it tightly like you do
when we're at the hospital.
you hate getting shots.
my focus shifts, but it remains on you.

sometimes my focus is to make you laugh
when you've got too much on your mind.
sometimes my focus is to make you feel better
when you can't seem to keep any food down.
episodes of *friends* and chicken noodle soup
usually do the trick.

sometimes my focus is to be quiet and let you let it all out.
i don't need to add my own stories, advice, jokes, etc.
i just let you fire away.
sometimes my focus is just to hug you
and let you know everything is going to work itself out.
my focus is something you always have,
and i can't help but to
pay attention to detail with you.

one more song.

i wish nights like these could last forever.
i wish the light switch would never be found
by a wandering hand.
i wish that mop heads would remain
resting in their buckets.
i wish that the couples around us would yawn more
and that their eyes would grow heavy.
i wish that their jackets would find their shoulders faster
and that their headlights would find
the highway leading them home.
i wish it was just you and i slow dancing on an empty floor.

we get these moments in places of practice.
tiny little moments on the hardwood floors of the living
room and mornings in the kitchen in our pajamas.
tonight, all of those little moments find each other
and merge into what we are now experiencing.
a seemingly endless euphoria with your hands in mine as
your head is buried in my chest.

the dj is long gone, and sam cooke is radiating from my
phone stuffed in my back pocket.
our steps are in unison and i'm trying to take as many
mental images of you as i can.
your brown hair flows down onto your shoulders
and graces your black dress.
your hazel eyes look up at me
with the hope and promise of infinite
"i love you's."

"it's almost midnight," you whisper.

"do you have an evil step-mother and step-sisters you need
to rush home to?"

"no, you goof," you say. "but it's getting late."

just one more song with you.
i need a little bit longer in this moment.

lost among the pages.

i didn't say a word.
i just plopped down next to you
and began to read.
i didn't want to say anything
(not that i knew the right words to say)
but i just needed you to know
that i was there for you.

sidewalk talks.

the leaves fall from the trees.
you kick through them as we walk.
i see that familiar look in your eyes.
you want to jump in them.
the bitterness of the wind may
cause my ball cap to fly off my noggin.
the high piles of snow may cause me to blaze
a trail for you to follow in.

"come on, bambi," i call out to you.
you give me a simple one-finger reply.

our breath may be visible as our faces
turn red from the cold.
i'll still walk you home.
even when it's well past midnight
and we thought we were cool
for staying out until bar close,

i'll still walk you home.

we may live many blocks apart from each other,
but it's worth the wear and tear on my shoes.
i can replace my shoes hundreds of times,
but nothing can replace
the precious sidewalk talks with you.

my scary movie.

there was a ghost that would follow me around
from room to room with every light i flipped.
she wouldn't make any sound,
but her presence was enough to
make me tremble and shake.

i would walk through the house
like a scared kid with a flashlight,
going to investigate the noise that came
from the basement.
i'd throw the covers over my head and pray
for her to just go away, but it was no use.

she would often hide in the closet;
guarding pictures and her belongings.

grabbing the louisville slugger resting at my bedside,
 i decided to eradicate this monster once and for all.

the house isn't haunted anymore,
but parts of town still are.

give and take.

take an extra scoop of coffee from the can for her
on the mornings when you know she'll need it.
drive up to the front door of the store
when the weather is bad and drop her off
while you go look for a parking spot.
take the time to let her know that
she is loved.

let her know she is loved
with the notes you leave on her car windshield.
let her know she is loved
with the blankets you place over her when she falls asleep
during another movie she picked out.
let her know she is loved
by cleaning the house while she catches up on *stranger things*.

take her to your church.
let the word of God lead you closer
to Him and to one another.

take time out of your busy schedules to go
on adventures together.
(yes, people over 20 years old can still have fun at arcades)

while you're doing all of this taking,
be sure not to take her heart for granted.
don't take it unless you
swear to protect it.

cuffing season.

it's always around this time of year that it happens.
there are so many future love stories
that i walk past every day.

it's fascinating if you stop and really think about it.
along with every car getting snow brushed off it,
there are two people introducing one another to
their families for the first time.

i think about stuff like how much a firm handshake means
to her father upon their first introduction.
i think about what jokes will be shared
at the dinner table about how one of them
brought home someone from college.
i think about what embarrassing stories will be told
from their childhoods.
what shade of red will their face turn?

homebody.

she's with her parents most nights
rather than out at the bars.
it's not that she doesn't drink her fair share
of alcohol filled fish bowls with friends,
but she values family time more than most.
even though she's heard the same stories
at the dinner table, she laughs
like someone is holding her down and tickling her.

"...so, we snuck through the woods to get to the barn party…"
her dad says as she scoots to the edge of the chair
she's leaned back into so many times.

she makes eye contact with her mother
who is finishing her tater tot hot dish
and smiling out of the corner of her mouth.

she knows there will come a day when these "date nights"
with her parents will end,
but right now she is more concerned about her father
trying to figure out google home.

simple reminders.

i find myself watching 80's romantic comedies often
just to remind myself that love is out there and exists.
although the love in those films is cheesy,
i'll take cheesy over feeling nothing.
i'll take a boombox held over my head over a text saying,
"i miss you."

i'll take conversations over walkie-talkie when a dm
would do the same job.

i'll take dancing and singing in a record store
over a snapchat.

i'll take a humorous romantic story
told by a grandpa to his sick grandson
over a subtweet.

sometimes cheesy and cliché is all you need to get you
through the hard times
...and maybe a great soundtrack too.

movie vending machine.

redbox movie nights keep me hopeful
when the work week gets long.
the cold seems to punch me in the face as i exit my truck.
the only defense that i have is the packers stocking cap
you bought me a couple of christmases ago
and a barely noticeable beard.
the cold is holding up well— "the beard"
...not so much.

as hammerheads pound nails into the boards,
it reminds me of the world war II reenactments we get
whenever we put a bag of popcorn in the microwave.
our dog will scoot off to the guest bedroom
and we'll try to time it out just right so
we don't burn it again.
we probably shouldn't have taken the chance at the thrift
store with this frankenstein of a microwave,
but it's a good conversation starter.
the half-gallon of cookie dough ice cream in the freezer
isn't a bad back up plan either.

i normally pick out two movies

on my way back from work.

one for you and one for me.

the picks i've been making lately haven't been too hot,

but i promise i will get better.

i mean, i am bound to get it right eventually.

only 7 hours left of work.

6 hours 59 minutes and 59 seconds.

6 hours 59 minutes and 58 seconds…

messages you'll never read.

my thumbs can't type out fast enough

the words i want to say.

they also can't hit the backspace button fast enough either.

little nudges.

she still waves at me.
she still smiles at me when i walk past her.
why? i don't deserve this kindness.
i don't deserve her grace.
wouldn't it be easier if she just ignored me?
it's been over a year and yet she's still is in my head
in-between sips of my coffee in the morning.

she's still the person i want to call when
good things are happening in my life.
from finding a $20 in an old pair of jeans
to getting the promotion i was hoping for at work.
she's still the instagram account i find myself scrolling
through late in the evening.
there's got to be a reason for this.
there's got to be a reason i haven't been able to erase her
memory.

i forget my keys.
i forget birthdays.
i forget where i put my wallet.
but i can't seem to forget her.

my actual day job.

your feet are cold,
but i welcome them to my side of the bed anyway.
your tv shows are way too predictable,
but i sit in silence and watch them anyway.

just to see you happy.

your friends talk way too fast for me to comprehend
what is being said, but it's probably better
that i don't know sometimes.
your favorite movies are the scary kind,
but i am still in the spot next to you
at the theater or on the couch.
i'll leave every light on in the house
as i bounce from room to room when i am home alone,
but i will be strong for you
—or at least pretend to be.

just to see you smile.

i know my idea of a great morning doesn't involve
waking up at 5a.m. to bring you to the airport,
but the face you make when i stop while you're sleeping
to pick up coffee and donuts is worth it.
(yes, waking up at 5a.m. is easier during hunting season.)

i may not always be ready for you
to take selfies of us together,
but i'll do my best to show those pearly whites.
"keep her smiling and laughing is your main job.
never take a day off,"
is what my grandpa once told me.
if that's my job, i never want to call in sick.
just don't ask me to do a powerpoint presentation.

monsters.

i'm not a monster,
but I feel like it sometimes when I look in the mirror.
this whole time i was searching for them under my bed
but was unaware there was one
inside me
whenever she stops coming around.

present.

we all try our best to say the perfect
"i love you."
the easiest way to show it is just by
showing up.

no roses or chocolates need to be in your hands.
no doves need to fly,
and no perfect soundtrack needs to be playing.

just be there.

be present.

let that person know that you're there for them
and you're not going anywhere.

railroad penguins.

we walk the train tracks at night.
we spread our arms out wide
as we try to keep our balance on the rails.
we are flightless birds,
but nights like these feel different.

the moon seems brighter and hangs in the sky
like a lantern to guide our path.
the stars seem to shoot
like we've captured a genie that grants us infinite wishes.
we whistle to songs that we've made up together
that often get cut short by our laughter and rosy cheeks.
we don't know where these tracks will take us,
we just listen for the train.

scenic route.

let us always take the scenic route.
when shortcuts would be quicker
and save us a few minutes,
let us take the winding back roads instead.
let us not be concerned with passing those around us
or maintaining a certain speed.
once we take the pedal off of the floor
and pump the brakes,
the drive seems sweeter.

we'll get to where we are going eventually, but let's

stop.

to enjoy the photo opportunities along the way.

walking with ghosts.

i examine these ghosts from my past
on these night walks that i take.
sometimes they are walks with an old friend
and sometimes it's as though
i'm walking next to an enemy.
these ghosts tell me
things i didn't know about myself before.
they tell me secrets that they've kept
inside for quite some time.

"why didn't you tell me sooner?" i ask.

"you never gave us the opportunity to speak," they reply.

falling slowly.

"i love sweatshirt weather,"
you say to me as we climb into the truck.
you take a big whiff of the autumn air.
you try to hold it in until we get out to the farm.
it's the taste of the caramel apples that gets me.
it's close to your kisses,
but your lips taste better than stringy caramel
that gets stuck to our faces.
we push each other into the corn and get looks from strangers,
but we don't mind them anymore than the scarecrows.

meeting my parents.

you check to see if your teeth are clean
in the camera on your phone.

"you're fine," i say, but you stick your jaw out
a little further anyways.

"i just want to make a good impression," you say,
"if i've got gunk in my teeth, then what does that say about me?"

you worry too much
about the non-existent food in your teeth,
the one strand of hair that's out of line,
your laugh being too loud,
and you running out of things to talk about.

"just be you," i tell you.
"you can mess up my hair if it will make you feel better."

i lean my head towards you. you raise your hand as if
you're going to go in for the kill, but you put it back on
your lap.

"they're going to love you."

anxiety.

i worry.

i worry about
my morning breath being too strong when you
roll over to my side of the bed.

i worry
that my car won't start on my way
to pick you up from work.

i worry
that i'll burn the house down if i try that new recipe
you shared with me on facebook.

i worry
that we won't be able to travel
to all of the places that you want to go.

i worry
that i'll lose you in an argument
that i never should've started.

i worry

that i won't be able to win you back.

i worry

that i'll never be the man i want to be.

"what are you thinking about?"

you ask me as i gaze up at the ceiling.

"nothing."

our fancy dinner dates.

"i bet you could blindfold me
and i'd know all of these wines," you said
as you set down the menu.

you pursed your lips together
and sat a little higher in your chair.
your nose growing like pinocchio's
as you pretended to look down on me.

"is that so?" i replied,
knowing as much about wine as i do cross stitching.

"yes, indeed," you said with the confidence
of a young girl that just learned
hot crossed buns on the piano.

i wanted to see you in action.

the dollars may be stuffed into my wallet
and the hours i log on my time card may be long,
but you don't get this kind of entertainment anywhere.

i ordered three different small glasses of wine.
using the napkins at our table,
i blindfolded you and watched the magic
unfold before my eyes.

you sipped each one and had this smirk on your face
as if you had taken this test before.
you continue to amaze me.
these feelings you give me are priceless.

scrubs.

we cross off items on our weekend to do list
like a vengeful english teacher with a red pen.
after we change out of our sunday's best,
we throw on our sweats and get to cleaning the house.

"i get to pick the music this time,"
you tell me as you look at my stack of records
and pretend they aren't attached to my soul.

you put on something new.
it's something i have never heard before,
but it gets my toe to tap.

i squeeze the windex
along to the faint beat I pick up on from the bathroom.
we clean because we want to,
not because your parents on their way over.
not because we are expecting company,
but because we take pride in our home.
we take pride in clean dishes drying off in the rack.
we take comfort in knowing that we got the dust out
from underneath the rugs in the living room.
some may call it o.c.d.
we call it just another sunday before the packers game.

just two kids.

i don't think we are crazy for spending our nights like this.
we snuck onto the high school football field with a cheap
bottle of wine, a blanket and a chance for a kiss.

i'm not sure what's so romantic about a football field,
but you asked me to take you on a
country-love-song kind of date.
we worked our way through that bottle
like we were racing against the clock.
we thought we heard someone coming,
so we hopped the fence and took off.

we found some abandoned bikes sitting next to a tree.
we thought twice about taking them, but you reached for
them first and i was just following your lead.
we'd come back to our car eventually, but not before
taking a ride around town.
we saw people we knew,
and they just shook their heads and waved.
it's what they've come to expect from us.

no stopwatch.

i've learned to take my time.
i'm taking my time with you.
my heart tells me to rush it
and give you all i've got
but i have my mind to thank
for what it knows
and what my heart does not.

the principles of a man in love.

i want to bring you flowers.
i want to hand them to you even though i may shake at the
sight of your beauty at the front door.
i want to open your car door.
i know that you can open it yourself,
but i was raised on certain principles.
principles that I don't want to stop following
anytime soon.

open the door,
walk on the sidewalk with the traffic on my side,
pay for the first meal,
lend you my coat,
walk you up to your front door,
call you up at the end of a good night
to hear about your day.

my principles may seem old and outdated
and i may not always get it right,
but i want you to know my intentions are true.

if you're looking for a one-night fling or a quick hookup,
i can promise you that's not the kind of man i am.
that isn't love to me and i wish i could be like
 those "other guys" sometimes
and not over think every move i make in love,
but i'm not.

some say i'm an old man stuck inside a 23-year-old's body,
and i hope to continue that growth in my life.
that doesn't mean i'm a member of the fun police.
i'm always down for spontaneous adventures and a good
slice of pizza at 2 a.m.

i'm tired of this run around, catch feelings for each other,
texting, sub-tweeting, and at the end of the day not
knowing where we stand.
my heart can't take that crap anymore.
i want someone that i can work for.
someone i can think about when that big project
or test is coming up, and just thinking about them puts my
mind at ease.

the love that keeps me hungry for more
and hungry for the word of the Lord.
i want to grow in Him alongside of her.
i know that time spent in scripture and talking it out will
pay huge dividends on how we love not only one another,
but our neighbors.

 i want the love that has people talking about how they
can't wait for the next meal at our house, or how they can't
wait to see us at the next town function.
that's the type of love i want.
i'm not expecting perfection and i'm not expecting there to
be no snags in the relationship.
that's unrealistic to put that sort of pressure on a woman.
especially her.
at the end of the day,
i just want to be her face to call home.

napkins.

i keep napkins in my pocket in case she spills again.
i keep them there in case the tears find her eyes.
i'll try to wipe them the best that i can,
but sometimes they find her cheeks too quickly
and i'm not fast enough.

sometimes it's because she hasn't
seen her friends in a while.
sometimes she just needs a phone call from her mother.
sometimes the pressure of work gets to be too much.
sometimes it's because i don't communicate
well enough with her.

it all adds up and the dam breaks.
here i am,
trying to soak up all the water
with a pocket full of napkins.

polaroid.

one day, it'll all make sense.
the picture is just a little fuzzy right now.
i try to shake it around as fast as i can,
but nothing seems to turn out.
the film flops back and forth
like i am integrating it in my basement.
i want it to bleed, but it's sworn to secrecy
no matter what i do to it.
no names are whispered and no whereabouts are hinted at.
silence is all it knows.

so here i sit,
waiting for things to develop.

colder weather.

my favorite sweatshirt has been yours
since the day you put it on.
even though you're out of my life,
it still belongs to you.
it's currently folded on my dresser
just waiting for you to put it back on.

WINTER.

i think too much.

snowflakes carry a love more magical than anything found
in any of cupid's arrows.
there's something peaceful and romantic about peeking
out the lightly frosted windows
that captures our hearts.

the dancing snowflakes seem
to give us courage to ask questions we are too afraid to ask
in the sunshine.

frost.

everybody's out there looking for somebody
to keep the embers in their heart stoked
when all the frost wants to do is take over.

back at your door.

i'll wait outside your door
with a cup of coffee just the way you like it
and with a muffin that's probably too sugary.

i'll wait outside your door with flowers that will need
to take a dip into a vase for your kitchen table.

i'll wait outside your door
with a box full of chocolates that are
just waiting to be eaten
while we watch another disney movie
that we can already quote word for word.

i'll wait outside your door
with a pile full of blankets
because we're about to construct
the most elaborate blanket fort
this side of the mississippi.

i'll wait outside your door
with my heart racing because
tonight's our anniversary.

i'll wait outside your door
with a hangover care package in my hands
because your girlfriends were back in town for the
weekend.

i'll wait outside your door
with words struggling to come out
because I hurt you in some way.

i'll wait outside your door
until you want to talk things out.
when a man meets a woman like you,
you're worth the wait.

the great indoors.

the weather reports are usually worth
throwing out along with everything else,
but tonight feels different.

i walked down to the grocery store and was able to find
the hidden treasure that was the last gallon of 2% milk.
there were a couple of dents in the container,
but it seemed okay to me.

when i got home, you were sitting on the couch wrapped
up in a blanket and sipping on a cup of hot chocolate.
you patted the spot next to you like you had been saving it
for me from the dog.
i slid the jug of milk into the fridge.
there was just enough room between the styrofoam
containers and your yogurts
that I was able to squeeze it in.

i plopped down beside you.

"i'm praying for a snow day," you said.

you piled your whipped cream a little too high
because some evidence was left on the tip of your nose.
sherlock took the night off and decided not to
mention it to you.

"i don't know," I replied.
"seems like they never get it right."
you wrapped the blankets around me like you were
comforting me after a tough little league game loss.

"believe," you said with a smile.
you went on to tell me all of the things we would do
if the snow kept us from escaping our apartment.
i could almost taste the warm cookies in my mouth.
on a day where nothing seems to be going on outside,
the great indoors with you captivate me.

what i see.

whether it's sunday morning sitting at the breakfast table,
munching on a bowl of frosted flakes with you
in our pajamas.
or it's a friday night and we're out on the town
—you're beautiful to me.

you're not something "i'd smash", but you're beautiful.
a woman i find elegance and grace in.
your outer appearance is one of those things that draws me
to you but doesn't even scratch the surface as to why
i find you beautiful.

i find beauty in your handwriting.
the way you dot your "i's" and cross your "t's".
i find beauty in your ability to care for those around you,
even if it means you'll be running a little behind.
i find beauty in how you laugh things off.
your laughter is the warm cup of coffee to my soul that
jolts me awake in the cold wisconsin winters.
i find beauty in the moments when i realize
you're human, too.

those moments when i come over
and a bottle of wine is almost empty,
a half-eaten pizza is on the coffee table
and you're having a movie night.
those moments when you seem to have taken on
the role of a new york city cab driver
as we make our way down the highway
to your parents' house.
(you can bet the "oh, Jesus" handle is in use.)

those moments when your sarcasm dosage is
a little higher than normal.
your beauty is so much more than what you see
in the mirror
or on your cell phone screen.
you'll never know just how beautiful you are to me.

you've got a way.

you've got a way of making me stay.
i could be running behind and in a mad scramble,
but all seems calm when you give me
that smile and tell me not to worry.
i wish i could stay home with you.

"i'll see you after work," you say and slap me on the butt.

you've got a way of leaving voicemails on my phone
that have no sense of direction at all
and it's one of the cutest things about you.

you'll be talking about your day and then out of nowhere
we somehow worked our way into
which pizza place is the best in town.
don't think i don't listen to your messages more than once,
because i definitely do.

you've got a way of making my shoulders numb.
whether it's a movie night on the couch
or when we are at the bar
and you've had a little too much to drink.

my shoulders must be the perfect pillows for you
to rest your head on.

i wouldn't have it any other way.
you've got a way with life that leaves me
on the edge of my seat as i shove fistfuls
of popcorn into my mouth,
eager to find out what happens next.

a collection of things you should never stop doing.

never stop telling her she's beautiful;
even when she's got an old ice cream bucket next to her bedside in case she has to throw up again.

"don't look at me," she says, but you bring her a glass of water, medicine, and stay by her side anyways.

never stop telling her she's smart;
even when she locks her keys in her car.
(it probably didn't help the situation when you started playing the *mission impossible* theme song as the two of you tried to break into her car.)

never stop holding her hand.
never stop opening her door.
never stop walking on the traffic side of the sidewalk;
even after a heavy rainfall.
she'll get a good laugh out of the wave that just hit you.
(try not to be too upset by it. it was funny.)

never stop trying to work things out;
even when you feel like all hope is lost.

never stop asking for her forgiveness and grace;
even when you don't deserve it.
never stop putting the Lord at the center
of your relationship.
never stop being a gentleman.

grow old together, but never grow up.

my christmas wish list.

they say, as you get older, your christmas wish list shrinks
to things no longer under the tree,
but who is around it.
they couldn't be more spot on.

the silence and contentment that fills the living room
as the fireplace glows and the lights on the tree sparkle
fills me up with joy.
it fills my soul up like a cup of hot chocolate
before i embark on a brisk walk to grab the mail at the end
of the driveway.

you begin to wish you had the things back
from your childhood.
not toys,

but people.

if i could spend christmas morning with family members
that have passed away,
you could bet i would be up all night
waiting in anticipation.
i would rush down the stairs in my pajamas
and sleepy eyes to see
the most beautiful people sitting at the couch.

if only i could ask santa for things like that.

blankets.

please stop making me blankets.
i know i complain about being cold at night,
but i can't accept your gift.
when you're here,
it's the warmest i have ever felt.
i find myself being warmer than the burnt pizza
still caked to my oven because we fell asleep on each other
while watching *the office.*
we awoke to the sound of the fire alarm and we discovered
a hot mess that was anything but a four-cheese pizza.

when you're gone,
the blanket no longer warms my body.
i shiver and shake when i'm under its cover.
i toss it into the corner of the room,
no longer do i want to look at it.
along with the lint that clings to the blanket,
it carries with it reminders.
these small reminders keep me up at night
there is still so much i don't know the answers to.
i still hang onto it though,

there are maybes in every knot that is tied to hold
the blanket together.
those "maybes" make it easier to reach for it on nights
when the heat no longer finds my room.

i know you're trying to be thoughtful,
but please stop making me blankets.

save me a spot.

save a spot for me.
at first, you do it unintentionally.
you sit by yourself at the coffee shop reading from a book you pulled out of your bag.
you sit by yourself on the couch with the glow of the tv bringing the only light to the room.

save a spot for me at the concert.
i want to scream at the top of my lungs with you.
save a spot for me at the restaurant you love to go to.
(you know, the place where you don't even need a menu anymore.)

save me a spot at the random table you've been assigned to at your college friend's wedding.
whether we are fake laughing at the terrible jokes being told by your friend's third cousin while we wait on dinner or spend the night turning loose on the dance floor.
it'll be a night to remember.

save a spot for me in the photo booth.
let's make weird faces together and share a kiss or two.
these pictures will soon be plastered onto our fridge,
so get used to the thought of seeing them every time you reach for the milk.
i hope they make you smile.

save me a spot on the couch.
i am coming into the living room
with a stockpile of junk food.

i feel like freakin' willy wonka.

save me a spot for all of these things,
but above all else,
save me a spot in your heart.
you've made room for others before,
but they never chose to sit down.
they were no shows.
if you save me that spot, that's where i will be.
i may do things from time to time that'll make this seat saving harder to do,
but don't give up on me just yet.

i'm coming.

christmas tree farm adventures.

lost amongst the trees:
that's where you'll find her.
she'll imagine each and every one placed in her living room
before she makes her selection.
she'll ask for your opinion,
but then she'll be quick to think out loud
and make her decision before you can utter a single word.

"too many dead spots. not full enough. not tall enough."

meanwhile, you're standing there with the rusty saw
she had you grab from the garage.
you're wondering if she was this picky
when deciding whether or not to go on a date with you.
(and to answer your question: yes.)
she'll decorate it from top to bottom.
lights will line the tree,
but only after you spend a solid half hour untangling them.

ornaments from the store and from her grade school days
will dangle from still thawing branches.
she puts the ones that she's proud of making
at the front side of the tree.

oddly enough, the one's with her face on them seem to
find the back side of the tree year after year.
her smile grows wide as christmas music plays
softly over the stereo while you place the star
on top of the tree.

no chair needed.

she's truly in her winter wonderland.

silent little messengers.

snowy nights are my favorite.
they are so silent that you're afraid to sneeze
and disturb the peace.

snow claims the sidewalks as their own and pile onto
cars occupying the streets
like a scrawny kid at the bottom of a dog pile.
flakes seem to latch onto every shingle on the roof.
whether you're looking out the window from a warm
embrace of a blanket or you're outside trying to catch
them on your tongue;
there's something magical about it.
not quite hogwarts magical,
but you feel as though
anything can happen for an evening.

in the morning, the magic will be gone
along with the snow that has been plowed from the streets.
but for one night, new hope is found.
maybe somebody will pay for your meal.
maybe you'll get a call from an old friend.
maybe she or he will text you from out of the blue.

maybe.

maybe.

maybe.

i'd like to think that with each snowflake

that flutters in the air,

maybes get added to the equation.

this is why i love those silent nights

it makes it easier to listen for the answers to the maybes.

cookie crumbs.

she enjoys long romantic walks
down the aisles of target.
she enjoys the foam that melted marshmallows make
in her hot chocolate.
she enjoys watching her brother's fake smile
when he opens up another pair of socks
from grandma for christmas.

"you can see such pain in his eyes,"
she chuckles as she hunches over and grabs my knee.

she's the kind of woman who probably should've
complained about getting cheesy broccoli soup instead of
the pancakes she ordered,
but she spoons in mouthfuls of the soup anyways.

she's the kind of woman that sticks around after church to
catch up with the elderly folks she hasn't seen since
last Sunday.

she's the kind of woman you hear new things about in
town and you find a new appreciation for her
through every conversation in line at the bank.

she has her flaws as well
and that's what i enjoy most about her.
i don't think i've ever seen someone
who struggles so immensely with parallel parking.

"don't say anything. you just keep your mouth shut,
mister," she tells me while performing the act.

i pretend to zip my mouth shut and just smile at her.
i wave to people i recognize walking on the sidewalk.
mrs. zimmerman begins to laugh hysterically,
but i discreetly motion her to move along.
i scan often to make sure the local paper isn't on the scene.
we'll laugh about it later i'm sure, but for now,
i'm getting the silent treatment.

i take her to the coffee shop
in hopes to be able to poke my head out of the dog house
sometime soon.

she enjoys all of these little things in life
like the crumbs on the floor
that get overlooked by everyone else.

i get down on my hands and knees
and begin to enjoy looking for crumbs as well.

if these walls could talk.

a tub of cookie dough ice cream rests in the freezer
just in case.
a bottle of wine is snuggling with
the leftover pizza in the fridge.
a blanket is sprawled out on the couch
like a best friend looking for a hug.
her slippers giggle to themselves as they eagerly wait
to tickle and warm her feet.

she doesn't always use these friends.
most nights she's playing music on
her legendary spotify playlist and dancing while she cooks.
most nights she's on the go and gets home late after a
night out with coworkers and friends.
most nights she's laughing to herself as text messages
and gifs seem to blow up her phone.

Beep.

Beep.

Beep.

Check what it says.
Laugh.
Set it down and go back to whatever it was she was doing.

Beep.

Beep.

Repeat.

then there are those nights when the beeps stop.
the music is off.
the oven is never turned on and no laughter is overheard.

it's just us.

the just-in-case-cookie-dough-ice-cream finds
its spoon companion.
the bottle of wine is released with the pop of a cork.
the leftover pizza warms up as the low hum of
the microwave fills the apartment.
the blanket gives all of the love it can give
with every thread in its existence.
the slippers comfort her feet like a home cooked meal
made by her mother.

we all do our part to let her know it's going to be okay.
most nights aren't like this, but when they are,
we give her all of the love she cannot find.

clueless.

i don't even know what her lips taste like
i never took the chance to kiss them.
i don't even know the softness of her hands
i never held them in mine.

are her feet so cold that they cause me to shiver
or are they filled with warmth as she places them onto mine?
i don't know.

does she sing in the shower or does she like it to be completely silent?
what food is her favorite to make after a good day?
does she call her mother or her father after a bad one?
i don't know.
i don't know.
i don't know.

i was set on my own narrative.
how can i be the antagonist in my own story?
maybe i'm not the writer of it after all.

no take backs.

i bought a headphone splitter so we could share
the full experience that is a big band sinatra song.
we never did end up sharing that experience,
but we did share other things.

we shared looks from across the room.
we shared pizza fries that greased our fingers and faces.
we shared good morning and good night texts
that caused us to squint as we looked at our screens.
we shared secrets that we kept close to our chests
until we felt the walls coming down.
all it takes is one act of selfishness and
nobody wants to share anything with you anymore.

both people want everything they gave back.
they want their time,
their money,
their kisses,
their notes and their stories.
(well, most of the time it's both people.)

there are some cases that are different.
sometimes things are held onto.

pictures stay in phones.

conversations over text get analyzed over and over again and never seem to get deleted.

presents and gifts remain hung on walls and rest on desks.

these things remain to serve as a reminder.

they keep them and pretend they don't bother them,

but inside it's killing them.

they will be revived eventually, but right now,

the morphine doesn't seem to help.

made from scratch.

he cooks for one.
most nights it's something simple like eggs, frozen pizza,
or grilled cheese.
the quicker the better so he can get back to watching his
shows or playing his video games.

then there are those nights when he slows things down.
groceries are picked up fresh from the market,
classical music is playing over the speaker he has,
and time seems to come to a standstill.

he takes his time cooking this meal.
he imagines nights
when he cooks for more than one mouth.
he pictures her sitting at the kitchen countertop,
slapping her hands to the beat of the music and wondering
if this meal is going to be as good as he says it is.

(God, he hopes so.)

he sweats while he waits for her to take that first bite.
he monitors her face closely like he's removing an item in
a game of *operation*.

"damn, this is good," she says.

all of those nights cooking for one
have been in preparation
for his favorite food critic—
her.

last words.

it's interesting the things you can't remember being said,
but you'll always remember
the last words a person ever says to you.

still trying to forget.

i wish i could drink you away.
that the alcohol touches my lips and serves
as a memory erasing kiss.
no such kiss exists.

my head still hurts in the morning and then i remember
all that i was trying to forget.
i wish i could find another woman to take home,
but that's just not my style.
i wish that i could wake up next to a stranger
and not think it was you,
but i can't.

her hair may be brown,
i still see blonde.
i still smell your perfume even if i were to soak my bed
in kerosene and light it on fire.
i hate her laugh because it's not yours.
i remove her hand from my chest
because it's not as soft as yours.
i hide my hoodies and toss her a shirt i've never worn.
i have no connection.

what a beautiful bandit.

stealer of ball caps, hoodies, flannels, cut offs, and covers
you don't even try to hide your identity.
your face is known throughout town
and graces pictures hung up in my room.

you're wanted by most men when you walk by,
but i am glad you only steal from me.
you pack heat when you rob me,
but your weapon isn't like any kind of caliber
i've shot before.
it comes in the form of a smile and a laugh
that makes me raise
my hands in surrender in a heartbeat.

most people would lock things up when a thief is around,
but i find myself leaving more and more unattended.

20/20

"you're the sweetest thing that i have ever seen,"
i whisper to you.

"you're full of it," you reply.

i'll always see you.
for once, i'm not messing around with you.
i'll see you when you're perched by the window
in your reading chair, the one with the green fleece blanket
draped over it.
you tend to lose yourself amongst the pages,
but i always end up finding you.
i'll see you when you walk into any room.
it most commonly is the restaurant on madison avenue,
the one that always gives you the extra slice of bacon.

forgive me if this offends you,
but i like seeing you lost sometimes.
i'll be hiding out in a booth, and i see you scanning with
those blue eyes of yours.
you remind me of robocop the way you scan the faces of
everyone, just searching for a man in a blue ball cap.
you may not see me, but i see you.

"why didn't you wave at me," you ask.

"watching you is more fun," i reply with a smile.

i'll see you when you want everyone in the room
to turn their heads.
i know this because the famous lipstick that finds your
wine glass comes out partnered with that black dress.
you know you're beautiful in it too
and have this sense of cockiness about you,
like you know something everybody else doesn't.
i love that about you. we tend to take more pictures on
nights like these and i don't mind.

i'll see you on those days when you don't want to be seen
by anyone in the world—even me.
you know those days when you're in your pajamas all day.
the days when you can't seem to keep any food down
and your hair is a mess.
(your words, not mine.)
seeing you on those days are most important to me. not
because i enjoy seeing you sick and in pain, but because
that's when i get to truly fulfill my promise to you
and love you through it all.

lying to myself.

"not again," i told myself,
"not again for a while."
but then i heard your laugh and saw your smile.
dear Lord, here we go again.

the girl at the bookstore.

she flips through the pages of the novels,
hungry to find satisfaction
in another piece of literature.

she catches my eyes and i'm wondering
if i should feed her or listen to
her stomach rumble
because she's being a picky eater.
she's the book i can't stop reading.

can't hold it in.

what if i never told you how i felt about you?
what if i kept it all to myself?
it seems crazy to me to never tell you about
how thankful i am for those nights
when i come home to you.
you're sitting cross-legged on the couch,
eagerly waiting to hit the play button so we can
keep chipping away at *friends*.

how could i not let you know about
those dimples of yours?
they present themselves often when we are sharing
our inside jokes at that coffee shop just off of grand street.
how can i hold it in that you're the most
intelligent woman i know?
the heaps of books by your bedside keep you company
on those cold winter nights.

how could i keep this all to myself?

the truth is—i can't.

i want to be able to show you every day with
little notes, heart-to-heart conversations while you're in the
bath and i'm sitting on the countertop.

never tell you?
i don't think i could hold my breath that long.

hiding in plain sight.

everybody wants to make sure you're doing okay,
but nobody wants to see you when you're sad.
you pretend everything is fine and smile
and you're just hoping you can keep it together
throughout the day.

"how's it going?"

"good! what about you?"

everything is fine.
everything is okay.
don't cry. not here. not now.
not in front of this person.

the worst dinner party i'll ever be invited to.

i imagine sitting at a table with them surrounding
and mocking me.
they sit there and eat their cake as I eat
the crow placed in front of me.

"how does it feel?" they'll ask.
"how does it feel when it happens to you?"

the boy who grew up that was used to opening his christmas presents at 5 a.m.

hurry up and get here.
we've got too much to talk about.
too many movie nights ahead of us.
too many weddings to attend together
too many sketchy hotel rooms to sleep in.
too many miles to put on our vehicles
too many strangers to meet.
too many inside jokes to construct.
too many birthdays to celebrate
too many hangovers to cure.
too many little moments together.

wavering.

the hardest things are always worth telling people.
they may not come out as well as we would like them to,
but the release of them is like lifting an open cardboard
box from the top of our closet.
things tend to come out and scatter themselves.
nothing falls to the floor gently.
loud thuds echo off of the floor
before we know what hit the ground.
but it's the first step in organizing.
it's an embrace of the chaos.
and then we start picking ourselves up.

stop carrying these boxes around with you,
pretending that you're okay.

a notebook in my hands.

i try to live my life more like jack pearson.
i try to show thoughtfulness
in the little and mundane tasks.
i want to be uncommon like him.
i hope to keep you guessing
and i plan to win you over each day.
i know I am flawed and not everything i say
will make a hallmark card,
but i will continue to try every day.

i try to live my life more like luke danes.
i want to live more ruggedly.
i want to meet you at your level of sarcasm
and be able to give it right back to you.
i want to make your breakfast in the mornings
and share cups of coffee with you.

i try to live my life like chandler bing.
i want our cheeks to hurt from laughter
when we are together.
i don't want to think as much and over analyze
when i am with you.

you see, i can keep trying to be these men in these
television shows that find my screens.
but in doing so,
i wouldn't be true to myself.
i will steal tiny wrinkles out of their playbooks,
but at the end of the day—you're getting me.
someone not worthy of being on tv,
but lucky enough to have you in this life.

unscripted.

convenience store thoughts.

loving her isn't convenient.
sometimes it requires you to stay up late and hold her hair
back as she becomes friends with
the toilet for the evening.

sometimes it causes you to change your plans.
sometimes it's waiting outside of a certain store and
making awkward small talk about this "darn wisconsin
weather" with a complete stranger.
sometimes it can have you apologizing for things
that aren't your fault.
sometimes saying you're sorry won't be enough.
loving her may not be convenient
but loving her isn't like picking up a snickers bar
at a kwik trip at 11 o'clock at night.

collecting.

i've been stockpiling double xl shirts for you.
the kind that extend just above your knees
ones that you can put on and wear to bed
on warm summer nights when we leave the windows open.
ones that you can curl up in and sit next to the fire with
when the snow bends the trees with its burden.
it's not that i don't want you stealing my favorite t-shirts
and leaving your scent all over them.
it's not like that at all.
i want you to feel like home
when you climb into these shirts.

on nights when the bed may feel a little colder
when i am not there,
i hope you find an extra rush of warmth from them.
although they may fade after cycles through the wash,
may their effect remain the same.
this night shirt collection of mine continues to grow
with every sporting event that my hand reaches higher
than the rest.
with every christmas that my grandparents forget
my t-shirt size.
i can't wait to see you in them.

your ways.

i'm sorry to bother you again
but i couldn't help but to notice:

-the way you carry yourself

-the way you crinkle your nose
and cock your head to the side

-the way you laugh incredibly hard at your own jokes

-the way you dance to michael jackson, even if it's only you singing along with your phone

-the way you flip your hair and tuck it under your hat

-the way your voice trails off from time to time when you're tired, but you're still trying to carry on a conversation

i'm sorry, but i couldn't help but to notice you.

downtown.

the night sky dangles over our heads
and it's toying with the idea of
sending us a shooting star.

"what would you wish for," you ask me
as you avoid stepping on the sidewalk cracks.

"i can't tell you, otherwise it won't come true," i reply.
you stamp your feet down right smack dab on a crack
sending shockwaves through the pavement.

"yeah," you say, "well, i just broke my mother's back then."
you tug on my t-shirt sleeve like you're interrogating me.
it's as though your "big break" as a private investigator
depends on getting this secret wish of mine out of me.

no good cop.
no bad cop.
just you.

up all nights.

i can't believe we stayed up all night
watching home videos.
i know i'm going to be dragging behind today.
i'll be yawning like an old hound dog on a front porch,
but i can't get enough of these up all nights with you.
as the hands on the clock continue to climb,
our conversations drift off into aimless debates.
we discuss what the best disney movies are
and what we would do if we had access to
a time traveling car.

"does it have to be a delorean?" you say
like i just told you that *grey's anatomy* has been cancelled.

"what if our time machine was a pt cruiser?"
i try to wrap my head around traveling through time
in a vehicle commonly found at bingo halls
and golf courses, but it just doesn't feel right.

we raid the pantry during these up all nights
and create these treats that bring us back
to our college days.

s'mores made with animal crackers, mini marshmallows,
a hershey's kiss and we are all set.
we eat like waistlines don't exist
and calories are mythical creation.
these nights end with us falling asleep on one another
with our mouths and hearts wide open.

finals week.

she fidgets with her cross necklace when she's nervous.
she tugs and pulls at it as if she'll free the cross from its chain at a moment's notice.
she slides it from side-to-side.
she scratches at her nail polish and picks away at it leaving only fragments of a paint job that was done in her bedroom just a few nights ago.
she sighs more often and twirls her hair with her finger like spaghetti noodles finding a fork.

"you're going to do great," i tell her and smile.

"you have to tell me that," she replies, "you're my boyfriend."

i scan the pile of textbooks in front of her
and the notecard that is shaking in her hands.
scribblings are everywhere, but from the little bit that i can make out, i am fairly certain she accidentally wrote down a recipe while writing it at 3a.m.
i decide not to mention it.

"just because i'm your boyfriend, it doesn't make it any less true."

she shakes her head and shows me that smile
that i fell in love with.
the one that i look forward to seeing come out of hiding
behind a "central perk" coffee cup.
the one that says, "i've been up to no good."
the smile that finds the pictures in my phone
from adventures we went on
when we should've been doing homework.

that smile is what i needed her to show me.
i needed to see that smile before
i left her to finish her last minute cramming.

someone like you.

someone like you is what i've been spending
so many nights praying for.

you unapologetically race up to my car door
with that wide smile holds me captive.
you're a trash talker when it comes to us playing basketball
in the driveway, board games at friends' houses, or when
we're wrapping presents for family members.
despite your competitiveness, you'll still be eager
to serve those around you.

you value our alone time, but you also enjoy when our
home is open, and meals are shared.

you always seem to see the silver linings in situations but
aren't afraid to admit when things just suck sometimes.
someone like you is what you'll find in my prayer journal.
you're written all over it.
in the margins and bleeding onto other pages.

i may get tired of things,
but i'll never get tired of praying for someone like you.

a simple prayer.

i hope we look like love when people see us together.
i hope they see us serving one another
in subtle ways each day.

i hope they see us serving those around us as well.
i hope they see us and think, "i want what they've got."
i hope our strength in our relationship comes from our
relationship with God.
that grace isn't just said before meals,
but before presentations, meetings, at the bus stop,
in the grocery store and on sidewalks.
may opportunities find us like a tap on the shoulder
and may our home be a welcoming place
that doesn't need tiny signs to say so.

life with you is going to be fun and filled with many
faith testing situations.
when these giants present themselves,
let us lean on our firm foundation in Him
to help see us through.

the magician.

card tricks are mere child's play.
i am far too advanced for my own well-being.
i'm past the days of pulling rabbits out of my top hat,
escaping handcuffs, and pulling quarters out
from behind people's ears.

i have the ability to make people disappear.
i do this unintentionally with the magic words that i utter,
the actions that i do and fail to do.

poof!

they're gone.

i still haven't figured out
how to bring them back.

outbursts.

wanting stuff you can't have
tends to hurt more as you grow older.
tantrums you once threw at the grocery store over a candy
bar seem like nothing now.
fits you'd have in the backseat of the car because you
called shotgun but your older sibling still managed
to claim "your spot".
you'd give anything to have again.

a later bedtime isn't something you'd argue over anymore
because you're lucky to get a few hours of sleep
this past week.
month.
year.

the perception of crying because you can't have what you
want has changed as well.
tears are what make you human.
it's okay to shed a few of them.
you find yourself doing a little more of that now.

certain songs will come on the radio.
certain tv shows and movies will trigger
something inside of you.
hell, sometimes it happens when
you're shopping for groceries.
most of all, it's that couple that always seems to be
next to you wherever you go.

and there you go again,
wanting what the neighbors have.

closed lips.

please don't tell her that i stopped by.
this used to be her favorite place to grab a cup of coffee.
we used to sit in the corner booth together discussing
how our favorite bands had changed over the years.
we would bad mouth our professors about all of the
homework they would load us up with on the weekends.
she would get a couple of cups into her system
and there was no stopping her once she got going.

"the caffeine has taken me hostage," she'd say
as she held out her shaking hand and laughed.

please don't tell her i still skip over to the next station
whenever our song comes on the radio.

"come on, that was a good one," my friend says in the car.

"I just wasn't feelin' it," i reply.

please don't tell her i almost called her last night.
my finger hovered over the call button
for what felt like an eternity before powering off my
phone.

please don't tell her that i stay out late at night
and look up at the moon and stars longer than i should.
she liked our night walks when we would talk about
where we'd travel to if money didn't matter.
she wanted to visit europe and take pictures
until her camera ran out of storage.
she wanted to eat food with bizarre names
and peer out of train windows while it was raining.
please don't tell her that i haven't seen anyone since her.
she's probably moved on by now and she thinks i should,
too.

please don't tell her that i still love her.
let me do that.

SPRING.

my favorite time of year.

it's almost sundress season.
she'll peel that yellow dress off the hanger in her closet,
and she'll smile wide, knowing wholeheartedly
what she's doing to me.

the sun will make sure it isn't behind the clouds that day.
it'll push them away like it's trying to
make its way through a crowded college bar.
it'll make sure it's out as soon as she opens her front door.
it'll follow her as she walks to class.
she'll admire it from the classroom window
and will long to feel its warmth on her skin.
when the sun is done taking her attention,
i hope to steal a few seconds of her time
just to tell her how beautiful she looks.

"i know," she replies and goes on reading her book
next to the river.

she glows like the candle that lights up the living room
when the power goes out during a storm.

i'm not saying that she isn't always
bringing light into my life,
but there's something special about
the first day she wears that dress.
it's as though the birds hold their breath,
the flowers wait to bloom, as if to say
she's the official start of spring.

sweet tooth.

she's terrible at keeping a straight face.
serious isn't in her vocabulary.
she's got that
spit-out-her-drink-trying-to-hold-in-a-laugh
way about her.

it's hard to be in a bad mood when you're in her presence.
she's the reason
you're filling up water balloons on a friday night
because she wants to have
a water balloon fight in the backyard.

she's the one to make faces back at the kid
in front of you at the checkout line.
she's the one that leaves your cheeks and sides aching
as you make up dance moves together
at your hometown festival.

she's the one that you wait for her smile in the morning
to peek out from her big blue coffee cup so that you can
start your day.

her bubbliness seems to work its way into
lazy sunday morning pillow talks involving
what you would do if hogwarts was real
and your hypothetical child received a letter.

she's the sugar to your kool-aid.
life with laughter and her
is sweeter than you ever could've imagined.
loving her makes you afraid to visit the dentist.

two of a kind.

"a bit different," is how most of the townspeople
would describe us.
we were the ones that were out past curfew as kids.
we were the climbers of water towers just to share a kiss.
we were the first ones on the dance floor
and the last ones left after everybody else had snuck out
to drink cheap beer in the woods.
we were the ones to stuff ourselves with greasy
cheeseburgers and whip donuts in a vacant parking lot
until one of us threw up.

as bills began finding our mailboxes
and time cards began getting punched,
we were still alone together on many excursions.

we're still the first ones in line
as a new disney movie hits theaters.
we're the ones spending evenings in the grocery store
making terrible jokes with product names.
we're the ones who keep our radio up
even when we pass the cops.

we're the yellow starburst to many people

because of this lifestyle we lead.

the weird looks bother us about as much as the problem

of having too many sprinkles on our donut.

being a bit different is what keeps us young.

we never even had to make a trip to neverland to do so.

back when we didn't have control of the camera.

the travel agent was wrong this year.
we didn't need to take a trip to italy to find each other.

to fall in love.

through the static of the vhs tape
and seeing you in your most innocent form,
i'm falling in love with you all over again.

you make fun of me
for my terrible dance moves that i was doing
while aaron carter played in the background.

"do the 'crazy legs' move," my father says
through the fractured audio.

"i'm totally asking you to break that move out
at the next wedding we're at," you say.

"i think that move has been retired," i reply as i reach for
another slice of pizza from the box.

i poke a little fun at you when the video of you putting on
your own makeup for the first time comes on.

"i was four years old, okay," you say
like you're on a late night trial.

"i'm glad you've figured it out since then," i say.

"well, thanks," you reply, giving me a half-hearted smile.

i pull you in close to me as we continue to watch
our childhood evolution take place.
we watch through the lens of twentysomethings with
still many home videos to make together.

broken volume knob.

don't text me
asking me if i'm up
when we haven't talked in weeks.

ask me to go to the record store
in the middle of the day instead.
i'll play you all of the music
that's been drowning out your voice
when the thoughts of you creep in.

easier isn't always better.

it's easier to call her crazy.
it's easier to put all of the blame on her.
it's easier to pretend like you did nothing wrong.
but it doesn't mean it's right.
i think playing the victim makes talking about it easier.
our friends will tell us what we want to hear when we say,
 "she was a bitch."

that feeling of ease is only temporary.
maybe the two of you weren't meant to be,
but instead of calling her every name under the sun,
take what you've learned and apply it moving forward.
you'll be a better man because of it.

things i tell myself to help fall asleep at night.

she'll get here when she gets here.

cover up.

you can go from showing your scars to people to not recognizing each other at a coffee shop faster than i thought.

unplugged.

my love for you
goes beyond the clever captions and hashtags.
it extends into dinner being on the table
when you come home.
your hand in mine as we walk the city streets.
my love for you reaches beyond the retweets and likes,
but presents itself in the form of massages,
sing along sessions in the car,
kisses on the forehead,
and a jacket placed on your shoulders.

other people see it, but it doesn't attach itself to a filter.
they see it in the way we look at and treat one another.
they see it in the playful trash talk
and the lip curls over your teeth
when we are up to no good together.
they see it with your hand in my back pocket and mine in yours.

it's social, but no media can capture it.
it has to be felt firsthand.

the gifts you keep giving me.

you'll never understand the way i need you
and that's okay.
i need to hear your stories from work
even if you think nothing eventful happened.
if i am preoccupied with something else,
shake me and tell me to wake up.
i'll go through this life in a daydream slumber
if I am not careful enough.

you'll never know how much i enjoy your company
when i'm grilling chicken and you're out on the porch
telling me about the book you just can't seem to put down.
you'll never know how much i enjoy our day off trips
to different spots to munch on a burger and crunchy fries.
you'll never know how you look to me
when we trap ourselves in a blanket fort
and watch harry potter movies all day long.
you'll never know how you awake my soul
when you pray over us before we fall asleep
with the windows open on a cloudless, summer night.
i can tell you all of these things and i do,
but there's still so much beauty i find in you
that I have trouble expressing it.

we never end up where we thought we'd be.

"we need to leave," you said at the restaurant that night.

"but we haven't even ordered yet," i replied as i set down my glass of water. you set down your menu after letting it conceal your face for so long. you practically swatted mine out of my hands.

"my boss is here," you whispered as if you were telling me a secret about your best friend being pregnant. "so, what?" i said. i didn't know you had called in sick today so that we could go hiking. you told me you were using a vacation day.

"we need to leave. now," you said while squeezing my knee for emphasis.

we bolted towards the door. i pretended to take a phone call, saying we were on our way to the hospital about as loudly as i could without drawing too much attention to us. (it wasn't one of my finer moments, but it's all i could think of at the time.) we ended up going through the dairy queen drive thru that night while dressed to the nines.

we drove out to a small private lake where an elderly man that i used to mow lawns for lived.

"you definitely took a lot of girls out here in high school, didn't you?" you asked.

"no..." i replied, but you knew damn well that i was lying through my oreo blizzard covered teeth.

we are more fun when we improvise.
we can make all of these plans and try to follow them, but then life happens.
we find ourselves dipping our feet into a duck itch infested shoreline when we should be eating overpriced fish.

senses.

i'm afraid of losing my sense of touch.
i worry about never being able to
feel your hand in mine again.

i worry about never being able to touch your face.
i'm afraid of losing my sense of smell;
even when your hair wraps itself around my face during a
movie marathon on the couch.
i still love the smell of it even as i pull strands off of my
clothes the next morning.

i'm afraid of losing my eyesight
so i try to take you in as long as i can.

"take a picture, it'll last longer," you say, but that's exactly
what i am doing.

i'm taking these mental photographs of you.
it's not only when you're dressed up, but also when we are
out on the lake and you make that terrified face when
we're going too fast.

i take them when we take our night walks and pretend
we're private investigators when we find a mysterious item
on the sidewalk.

i take them when we are out on the front porch
with leon bridges playing over the speaker
and we have our faces in books.
i can never have enough.

i'm afraid of losing my hearing.
it's not just because i love music, but i'd miss out on the
many sounds you make.
the sound you make
when you stretch yourself awake in the mornings.
the sound you make
when the pizza timer goes off and you rush to the kitchen.
your laugh when you're laughing at your own jokes.
your shiver sound you make when the car is too cold on
those early december mornings.
may i never have headphones on when you're around.

the final sense i wouldn't want to lose is taste.

it's not just because i'd miss your kisses,

but i'd miss our meals together.

the meals from the drive thrus and the ones around the dinner table during the holidays.

these senses are something I never hope to lose.

i'd be losing a little bit of you with every sense that vanished.

this table.

coffee cups are scattered in the sink.
our mornings are spent at the table with forks scraping our plates as we shovel scrambled eggs into our mouths before we begin our day.

we take these simple mornings before the rest of the world is awake to spend time lost in the scriptures and in prayer. whatever chaos may be happening in our work lives that causes us to worry about early gray hairs setting in seems to get worked out at this table.

it gets prayed for.

whatever turmoil that creeps up in our friends' lives when they can't bear the burden alone anymore gets prayed for.

more plates are set down for dinner at night.

whatever may be causing a riff in our lives and relationship gets settled at this table.
we talk through these barriers that seem to place themselves in front of us.

we hop over these hurdles together.
the barriers are shape shifters and take different forms.

bills.
lack of communication about our schedules.
whose turn it is to take out the trash.
why was this item left out for the umpteenth time.

this table has gotten us through the toughest of times and
as long as there is always a spot for God to sit at it,
there's no reason for me to believe that i'll ever be sitting
at this table alone.

just because it's tuesday.

the best money i spend is on those little items
that make me think of you.

tongue tied.

i trip over my words when i am around you.
it's not that i have this constant anxiety or nervousness,
but there's so much i want to tell you.

it's so much more than telling you that you're beautiful,
but it's telling you about how i enjoy finding your
handwritten notes on the counter in the morning.
i want to tell you that i agree with
your opinion about that art piece we saw.
i want to tell you about the ice cream
residing in the corner of your mouth that you didn't notice
was there, or maybe you're testing me.

i want to say all of these things.

love i you.
you love i.
i love you.

there.
finally, i was able to tell you what i wanted to.

exposure.

there aren't many days that go by
that i don't think about you.
you'd think by now that i'd have it all figured out,
but i'm still going through hell.
i don't numb my mind with whiskey,
for it only gets me through the nights.
the times which are the toughest are
when i turn on all of the lights.

the difference.

the difference between a boy and a man sometimes comes
down to something as simple as a handshake.
a phone call instead of a text.
a knock on a front door instead of a honk of the horn.
a savings account instead of a coffee can
on top of the fridge.
dishes in the drying rack instead of another
crumpled receipt in the wastebasket.

the differences are often subtle,
but make a profound impact
when she walks into your life.

maestro.

your dress was playing a lavender lullaby for me
as it swayed to the wind's slow waltz.
i was mesmerized with how quickly you changed
the pace of my

kick.
drum.
heart.

you form strong crescendos whenever you're near me.
when you're gone, i must focus my full attention
in order to find the beat again.
you tote a full orchestra without ever realizing
the music you're making.

downpour.

from the inside of my car
it seems as though we're trapped.
the rain holds us hostage and by the looks of things,
we're going to be in here a while.

the drops of water hit the windshield so angrily.
we are being punished
for cheating on it with the sunshine.
how fruitful this forbidden love was.
mother nature is finally getting her revenge
for we spent too many days with the windows rolled down
on the journeys we took to little ma and pop restaurants
that had yet to tickle our taste buds.

we spent too many 75-degree days
sipping on gas station slushies and walking
to concerts in the park.

we spent too many cloudless starry nights
around a campfire with sticky fingers
while swatting away at the smoke that always followed us.

a downpour was sure to find us eventually.

rain is often associated with gloom
like dead flowers sitting in a vase on the kitchen counter.
we don't view rain as this never-ending depression,
but more as a new opportunity to reconnect.

"do you want to go out and dance in this storm?"
i ask as i motion my head towards the car door.

"you know me better than that," you said,
"i'm staying warm in here, but i like the way you think."

i didn't really want to go out in the storm either,
but i figured i would offer up a little adventure.
wherever you go—i'll follow.
even in the midst of the thunderstorms that find us.

strangers with our camera.

"can you take a picture for us," you asked
the man next to us on the streets of london.

"you know we could always take a selfie,"
i say while you fix your hair for the perfect pose.

"yeah, but a selfie doesn't allow you to make a connection
with a complete stranger," you reply.

i must admit that you keep me on my toes.
this stranger snaps a photo of us
and doesn't think anything of it.
they'll go about the rest of their day.
it won't come up in dinner conversation about
how their day was
or if anything interesting happened.
it was just the polite thing to do.
it was just another picture.

but not to us.

to us, this was a moment in time when we felt the urge to
follow our hearts with our passports and plane tickets.
we scrapped up what we could and spent less
nights out with friends.
we spent more time making cheap home cooked meals
and eating pb&js.

was it worth it?
absolutely.

gaze.

your eyes tell me all i need to know.
they're so easy to get lost in when we talk.
i like to witness how they expand
when you're excited about something.
we keep eye contact and are drawn into one another
by this invisible string.
it pushes us forwards and backwards in our chairs
with both intrigue and laughter.
our coffee has grown cold by the time
we finally get to sipping it.
there are bigger problems that i face
than wasting a cup of the finest joe.

those eyes haunt me in delight,
because I never asked for your number.

conversations with myself about her

the universe will find a way to bring us back together.
i just know it will.

something to come back to.

i take the longer walks home.
not because i have the time to spare
because there are plenty of other things i should be doing.
my homework still waits up for me
like an anxious mother does on friday nights
when it's getting close to curfew.
the dishes still need to soak.
those books that sit on my shelf need to be read.
those netflix shows need to be binge watched.

it's all gotta get done.
nothing can wait.
one task completed,
now onto the next one.
red light. green light. go. go. go.

the long walks home provide me a time
to chew the food from the day.
some of the realities are a little harder
to swallow than others.
they are eventually digested as i stop at a bench
and wait for a wise old man to sit down next to me,
but one never appears.

we're not hipsters.

the drive-in movie theaters are all closing down.
the silver screens illuminate faces in front seats
and in the beds of pickup trucks.
blankets keep us cozy and also help conceal
a $9 bottle of wine.
we sneak sips like our high school athletic careers
depended on it despite the fact that we've hung up our
letterman's jackets years ago.
our nights here will soon be over thanks to netflix and
other killers of social cinema.

the record stores are closing their shop doors.
needles will soon find dust caking their ability to get
someone through a heartbreak
or to help a young couple fall in love.
we still keep the vinyl heartbeat alive and well within our
tiny apartment on brackett ave.

i wouldn't necessarily call us "hipsters" but rather
 "preservers of the good things in life."

no golden boy.

why would a woman like you ever talk to a guy like me?
i haven't shaved in a few weeks and my scruff
is starting to take over my face.

the last time i went for a run was for beer
when we ran out while watching the badgers game.
you should've seen the hero's welcome i received
when i came back from the gas station down on birch
street.

i don't remember the last meal i ate
that wasn't made out of a box.
i still find myself throwing out the cooking instructions
before i'm done cooking and having to rifle through the
garbage to double check the directions.

i am not rolling in the dough by any means
and i will probably work until they put me in the ground.
after all of these faults, you're still sitting before me
and haven't rushed out of the door yet
for reasons that i am longing to find out.

another first date.

she looked too much like you.
it's all i saw staring back at me
that whole evening at dinner.
our conversations were short and didactic.

"what's your major?"
"who's your favorite professor?"
"what do you do for fun on the weekends?"

i might as well have brought up the weather.
i didn't kiss her goodnight
because i didn't feel like gambling.
i kept my chips in my pocket, folded, and gave her a hug.

a freakin' hug.

a request.

i can tell you that i've changed,
but you probably wouldn't believe me.
i can tell you that i haven't packed my schedule as much
and that you'd be my number one priority,
but you probably wouldn't believe me.
i can tell you that i've grown up
and don't stay out as late anymore,
but you probably wouldn't believe me.
i can tell you that i've spend more time
on my knees talking to God.
i can tell you that i've learned how to cook
and that i clean up after myself.
i can tell you that i've updated my wardrobe
and those funny shirts no longer fill my dresser drawers.
i can tell you that i miss hearing your laugh
and seeing your smile.
i can tell you that i haven't kissed anyone since you.
i can talk until i pass out, but i must show you.

let me show you that i've changed.

confessions of a dj.

i fell in love with you on the dance floor that night.
i know that i should've just stuck to playing my music
and nodding my head to the beat,
but I let my eyes wander.
i fell in love with the way you moved
and the way you belted out those song lyrics.

"am i more than you bargained for…"

as the night wore on, i came to the realization that our
time together was coming to a close.
they'd soon be wiping down the tables
and vacuums would begin to hum.
my cords would find my plastic cases and my speakers
would be laid to rest in the backseat of my car.
i'd drive home in silence to give my ears a break.

our night was going to be over soon and so was this love.
you probably had a boyfriend to go home to and i found
myself having to fall out of love with you as you left.

that smile had to lose its charm.
that blue dress didn't look *all* that pretty.
your laugh was *really* annoying.
your voice wasn't *that* soft,
and i definitely couldn't get used to it saying,
 "good morning" and "good night."

i tell myself these lies to help me fall asleep at night,
all while you were dancing away with my heart.

be honest with me.

you worry about your imperfections too much. stop it.
eat that cupcake that's catching your eye.
i mean, you can share it with me if you want,
but go for it, honey.

your hair doesn't need to look like hers to make me happy.
i love you with your hair down, tied up, smelling like
watermelons or whatever the heck they can capture
and put into that bottle.
i love your hair under a ball cap, or with a marshmallow in
it because someone got a little antsy next to the fire.

you're the woman i love and you're beautiful,
but you scare me when you turn into
the tequila monster after a night out with friends.

(what? i'm just shooting you straight like you asked.)

but in all honesty, you're way out of my league,
i can't imagine waking up next to anybody else
morning breath and all.

darty season.

i'm not sure how one gets a pretty woman to talk to him in a throwback nba jersey, but you started talking to me first. i was embracing my role as the "father of the house" and was monitoring the meat on the grill when you walked up with a grin, like you had a secret you just couldn't wait to blurt out.

"you're burning the burgers," you said and started swatting away at the smoke in the air.

"you think so? maybe that's the way i like 'em," i replied as i squeezed the tongs together. (that's the first thing they teach you when you're learning to become a grill master. clap the tongs together to let people know what you're all about.)

you reached for a bun and ripped it open.

"throw it in there," you requested. "let me taste test it. i'd hate for you to lose your street cred because you burnt the burgers and ruined everyone's lives." you held open the bun in your hands and looked up at me with your "well, i'm-waiting" eyes.

i reluctantly placed the burger down and awaited your review. gordon ramsey could've been standing before me and i would've been less nervous. you took a bite and i waited. you held up a finger.

"one: that's hot," you said as if you were trying to cool down a piece of charcoal in your mouth. you then held up another finger.

"two: that's delicious." i looked up to the sky and thanked God for allowing me to live to see another day. i wanted to say, "you could have these delicious burgers for the rest of your life. marry me," but what i actually said was, "and you thought they were burnt?"

you gave me a little shove and a closed lipped smile while knowing wholeheartedly that you had burger in the corners of your cheeks. our life started together that saturday, but i can't help but to think, what if i had actually burnt that burger but you were just too nice to say anything.

whether.

whether you spend thirty seconds
or thirty minutes in front of the mirror,
you'll never know how your beauty radiates.

whether you order a tiny salad
or a gigantic bacon cheeseburger,
my appetite for you is the same.

whether you know the score of the game or not,
i don't mind.
(actually, that's a lie.)
i do care.
this is a huge game
and i am glad you're watching it with me.

whether we've got a busy schedule
or a lazy, rainy sunday afternoon to kill,
it's always better with you.

sweet serendipity.

you're the woman i never knew i needed.
i was so set on my routine that i never went out
of my way to even try a new flavor of coffee.
i give the barista exact change every time
and then I carry on with my schedule.
i read for a while, i write, scroll through social media,
and then leave the coffee shop.
i never penciled you in.
you're a schedule and routine wrecker.

you add a little chaos to my life
like squirting ketchup onto macaroni and cheese.
you're an early riser and poke me until i wake up.
the sun's not even awake yet, so why do i have to be?

 "come on, think of how great that bacon is going to taste after a nice run," you tell me as you threaten to pounce on the bed.

"i'm up! i'm up!" i exclaim as i try to get on your level (which is damn near impossible if i may add).

you're the woman i never knew i needed,

the smile that i never knew i'd miss

during the middle of the day,

the spot on the couch i knew i'd need to make room for,

the shotgun rider that sings along to almost every song,

the eager reader that keeps feeding me books,

the conversation starter and ender, and

my forever woman.

i believe.

"what do you believe?"

i believe that the way someone looks into your eyes
 tells you a lot about that person.
i believe in the power of a long walk at night
and the good conversations that come with you
on the sidewalk.
i believe that sharing earbuds is a gesture that's underrated.
you want someone to experience a song the same way you
do, which is an unrealistic expectation to set,
but it's worth giving a shot.
i believe in handwritten letters and that they mean so much
more than any text message
or snapchat you could ever send.

i believe that the way you treat your mother and your
sisters says a lot about how you'll treat a woman.
i believe that a good home cooked meal
can bridge gaps between people.
i believe in long phone calls,
even when you've got nothing to say.
i believe in tipping your servers well and treating them with
respect.

i believe that the right woman will come into my life based on the Lord's timing and the moving of my feet.

i believe that old school still exists.

it's yours.

take my jacket when you're shivering.
take my ball cap when the sunlight
won't stay out of your eyes.
take my flannels off of their hangers
because you like the way my cologne lingers on them.
take a little food off of my plate if you feel like it, but
please allow me to do the same.
take my sweatshirts because you wanted
something to sleep in.
take my hand and lead me out onto the dance floor.
take my time as much as you want.
it's all yours.

study sessions.

you put your head on my shoulder
as you try to do your homework.
we've spent a solid two hours at this coffee shop,
yet we've somehow managed to get
absolutely zero homework done.

we're sharing headphones
and have to constantly monitor ourselves to make sure we
don't burst out into song and dance.

"just this once," i plead, "they'll think we're a flash mob
or something." you prop yourself up and look me in the
eyes.

"a flash mob of two," you raise your eyebrows, "keep
reading your book, vanilla ice," you say as you playfully
press my book into my chest.

we eventually get some work done,
but not without refills and snack breaks.

"i've *got* to finish this paper today,"
you tell me like i just sat down
and missed the first five minutes of the movie.

i love watching you when you get "in the zone."
you tie your hair up, bite down on your pencil from time
to time, and squirm in your seat.
you get these rushes of energy
like you're on the brink of a medical discovery
and i begin to fear for the livelihood of your laptop.
you come back down to reality after a while
and let out a sigh loud enough to make yourself
a studio audience of one.
i take these moments to watch you as a brain break,
and lately i haven't been turning in any assignments on
time.

the easiest thing you've ever asked me.

"tell me something you love about me," you say.

is this a trap? i think to myself.
but i find myself quickly responding to you.

i love it when your tongue curls over your teeth
when you're at your happiest.
sometimes it shows up when
something comes from the television.
sometimes it makes an appearance when
we're people watching while shopping at walmart
on a sunday afternoon.
i've noticed it comes out more
when i make a fool of myself.
for example: when i'm trying to coral the cheese
sliding off of my pizza,
but it looks like i am a baby deer
experiencing a drink of water for the first time.

or when i tried dancing to "god's plan" at the bar.
or when i let that fish go too soon
and it flopped into my shirt.

i don't get tired of this smile

and i hope to see it more and more,

like sunshine in a weather forecast.

may i make a fool of myself more often than not

and keep you smiling

as if it's all you know how to do around me.

smarty pants.

intelligence is sexy.
despite what you've been told about the girl with the
glasses and a book in her hands.
she hungers for more information and the answers to her
questions like a biker carbo loading before a big race.
(not chicken-alfredo-michael-scott carbo loading though.
that's a no-no.)

through this information she gathers,
she knows not only learns more about the world,
but also herself.
she takes different adventures all from the comfort of a
hammock rocking in the wind or on the boat in between
casts while the two of you are out fishing.

she enjoys the questions that create
discussion amongst many people.
the kind you have whether you're in a classroom setting,
dinner table, or around a campfire.

don't confuse intelligence with being uptight.
she's never met a board game that she didn't like
paired with a few glasses of wine.

she still sticks her tongue out in photos
and pours cold water on you from time to time
when you're in the shower.
she's the page turner, hand raiser and hell raiser
all mixed into one crazy, beautiful, and smart woman.

hands in my pocket.

i wanted to reach out and grab your hand that night,
but i know that i would be reaching for
much more than that.
i would be reaching for nighttime walks,
long hugs, meals shared across from each other,
day trips down to the lake for a swim and some fishing,
love letters tucked into mailboxes,
and slow dances in the middle of the street.

i would be reaching for your heart.
i would hold it in my hands, breathe into it and warm it up.
but i wasn't sure if you were ready for that yet,
so i just kept my hands in my pockets
and watched the rest of the movie.

unanswered questions.

how do you tell a woman you're crazy about her?
is it as easy as telling her that her shoe is untied
or that she needs to make a right turn
 at the next stop sign?
is it as easy as telling her she's got something in her eyes
or that there's a bug on her shirt?

no, it's difficult.

telling her is like climbing up to the highest point
at the old mining shaft,
accepting that triple-dog-dare, and jumping into the water.
it'll cause a lump to form in your throat.
one that you can't seem to swallow.
your hands will shake, and your knees will rattle.
you feel like you're attending your own funeral
as soon as you begin to speak.
words don't come out as easily as they used to,
but you've got to pull them out of you.

tell her how she makes you feel when you're around her.
tell her about the things that reminded you of her
that happened in the middle of the day.

tell her about the book she recommended to you
and about the show she told you to watch.
tell her about those sleepless nights.
speak from that 808 that is beating inside of your chest
and lay it all out on the table.
there's no one way to tell her you're crazy about her

but imagine if you don't.

thoughts before asking a cute girl out.

what i say today could change it all
or it could change nothing.

but i try not to think about the rain cloud
that could follow me home.
i would much rather think about the sunshine
and its rays reflecting off of my sunglasses.
i would much rather think about giving high fives to
strangers and the happy song playing through my
headphones.

i would much rather think about the dance moves
that i may or may not try on the sidewalk.
these thoughts are the ones that fill me up as i make my
way towards her, but droplets of doubt start to sprinkle.

oh, how i wish i had an umbrella handy sometimes.

rubix cube woman.

there's beauty in her complexity.
the more i try to understand her,
the less conclusions i am able to make.
to try to contain her is to be a fool.

she's free like the waves that rock our canoe.
she is ever-flowing.
you must take your time to get to know her.
surface level questions will not do the trick.

she likes to ask the
up-to-your-elbow-in-the-cookie-jar deep questions.
these questions you will have to ponder for a while.
it already takes you long enough to select
a box of cereal at the grocery store,
so answering her questions won't come easily.

you'll come to find that through these conversations
you'll not only get to know her better,
but you'll come to know the man you are,
the man you were, and the man you're becoming.

most men fear an intellectual woman,
but fear not, brave soul.
she's worth the long stares off into the distance
as you begin to question your mere existence.

hey, jealousy.

i'm spending too much time thinking about a woman that's out of my league.

she'll probably break my heart, but i am too blind to see the writing that is written on the wall.
she steals my attention, which is something that i will never get back like a cd or good book lent to a friend.
i know it'll freakin' crush me when i find out that she's got a boyfriend.

i hate a person that i've never met just because he's the one that gets to hold her hand and kiss her goodnight.
he's probably a great guy that walks dogs for the humane society, sings in the church worship band, and coaches a little league team.

but it helps me to picture him as a jerk and that i could treat her better.

how you'll know.

everybody has a different story of how
it happened to them.
there's always that moment they'll look back on.
the night they met and where they were,
but when did they know it was love?
how did they know they were in love?

you find the love in different ways.

once the "honeymoon stage" has worn off,
where do you see the love?

you see it when the two of you get home late from work
but join each other at the kitchen table for a bowl of cereal
to catch up on each other's day.

you see it when she makes the effort
to listen to your favorite band,
even though she's a little hesitant.

you see it when you make her favorite meal,
when she's had a bad day, or is laid up in bed with a fever.

it's in the candid moments.
it's found on the side of the road replacing a flat tire.
it's found when your gps is on the fritz
in the heart of the city.
in the rainstorms that come out of nowhere.
in the pictures you didn't know were being taken.

it'll show up in the form of laughter in seemingly serious moments, tickets to the game just because it's wednesday, notes left on the counter, dishes put back into the cupboards, a mixed cd in your work bag, home movie nights, conversations on the front porch, nights on a hill overlooking the city and not wanting to be anywhere else.

you'll find it.
it'll find you.
you'll give and receive it.

there's no greater gift exchange
that you'll ever be a part of.

we should be asleep.

it's late in the evening with our phones near our faces.
we open our heart and say things
we never thought we could.
but an answered text leaves us sleepless
throughout the night
and wondering.

did the they fall asleep or did i just mess everything up.

SUMMER.

if you really want to know what it's like.

I'm standing at the edge of the dock
watching the sunset and listening
to the loons carry a dinner conversation when she
shoves me into the lake.
it's a shock to my system, followed by laughter
when i finally resurface.

she's hunched over, barely breathing
while she laughs and waves a towel in the air.
water drips onto the wooden dock
as i prop myself back up
and snatch the towel from her hands.

i pretend like i'm mad at her,
but she sees right through it in a heartbeat.

"that was funny, and you know it," she says.

i smile and shake my head not knowing
if i should try to toss her in
or to let it be.

loving her is like
pulling the e-brake of your car in a high school parking lot
after a fresh snowfall.

it's spontaneous.

it's "i wonder what it would be like
to sneak into the neighbor's hot tub,"
and then actually going through with it.
it's grabbing dairy queen and going to cheer on
a random little league team together.

loving her is like throwing out your daily planner
but looking forward to the uncertainty
with each date that arrives.

doing what she likes.

she asks me to run a bath for her as she grabs
leftover cheese pizza from the fridge.
i make sure i pour in extra bubbles
because i get a kick out of her peering through
the mountain-like heap.
i pop in a norah jones cd into the boombox
in the corner of the bathroom
and set the volume at a solid six.
i do this, so i can hear her
when she starts to sing along.

"you're all set," i say to her.
we exchange places as she heads into the bathroom
and i into the kitchen.

she doesn't know it yet,
but i threw a little jimmy eat world on that
norah jones mix cd.

(what? i've got to keep her on her toes.)

i'm sitting at the kitchen counter when i hear her
start to sing melodies soft and sweet.
i swear it's like weaving cotton candy between my ears.
i hear her call for me and i set my drink down on the table.
i open the door and peek my head through.
she's eating her pizza as the bubbles have consumed her
entire body.

"read to me, please," she says.

i rush back to the bedroom and grab her book
that rests on her nightstand.
as we turn the pages and the story continues to unfold,
so does ours.

silent cues.

he was her easy button.
the one she looked to and felt relaxation with.
there would be days when she'd come home after being
fed to the wolves at work and just fall into his arms.
she had taken up a residency there.
it's where she wanted all of her mail sent.
the smell of his cologne would linger around her nose
and make her feel at home.
she would soak it up and take it all in
like she was smelling her mom's famous apple pie.

she didn't ask him to make dinner,
but he did anyways.
she didn't ask him to give her a neck massage
as she was catching up on *this is us*,
but he did anyways.
she didn't ask him to get tickets to the concert,
but he did anyways.

don't get it twisted,

there are plenty of days when she's his easy button,

but it's not a competition.

it's a common goal shared between them.

they want to carry the load together.

nobody like you.

i don't believe that anybody could love me like you can.
nobody can make random trips to target
as fun as you make them.
we go there needing like two things,
and we somehow kill a whole sunday by pretending
we were time travelers who have never experienced
a super target before.

the weird looks no longer seem to faze us.
nobody can make garage sales as fun as you.
we end up taking the most random trinkets home
after you have bartered like we are in chinatown.

"what are you going to do with that?" i say.

you shrug your shoulders and say, "i'll figure it out."

nobody can make power cleaning the house fun before
company comes over like you.
i don't think i have ever heard panic! at the disco played at
such a high volume before, but you fly around the house
while feeling the music.

i'm not entirely sure how much cleaning
is getting done between us,
but i couldn't care less.

not one of these things have happened yet
and i'm still ordering take out for one
but daydreaming about you gives me some hope.

adventure time.

i'll be your ticket when you need an escape.
pick out a spot on the map with your finger.
whether i've heard of the spot or not,
we'll get there.
it could be a day long road trip
just to get the heck out of town.

we'll pack our own lunches and find a scenic place
to gobble down our sandwiches.
we may spend most of our time fighting off bugs
that attack our blanket,
but it's the thought that counts, right?

we may be counting pennies at the kitchen counter,
but we'll find a way to get there.
we'll pick up extra shifts where we can,
and we may have to sell a few things on ebay,
but i promise you we will reach our destination eventually.
grab the map out of the glove box and close your eyes,
it's time for an adventure.

fishing buddy.

i look out at that fishing boat
sitting in the drive and imagine us in it.

we'll pick up a container of night crawlers from
the bait shop off of railroad street.
they will wriggle around in our fingers
and try to squirm away from us.

"you're just going to eat a sandwich after putting
your hand into that worm dirt," you say.

"my apologies," i reply as i dip my hands
into the water to wash them off.

you crinkle your nose and give me a smirk
before splashing a little flowage water in my face.
we will spend the day with our lines in the water
while we munch on snacks we raided from the pantry.
pop tarts, pringles, and trail mix.

it won't be easy fixing up that boat, but the best things in
life take a little elbow grease to truly enjoy.

homesick.

the texts no longer do it for me.
the phone calls only get me through until
the next time i see you.

i'm homesick.

my home is a mobile one.
it goes wherever you go.
it could be high in the new york skyline
or tucked back in the woods in a cabin with a fireplace.
i get glimpses of my home through the pictures you send.
through the voicemails you leave.
through the letters in the mail with your handwriting
beautifully gracing the pieces of crinkled notebook paper.

you've got the keys to my place
and only you know where they're at.

payments.

i'm in debt.
i keep getting calls and letters in the mail
asking for more.
i can't stop spending.

i can never repay you
for the love that you've given me.
i pull out crinkled ones from my pocket
and empty my change jar
whenever you come around.

it feels like i'm always broke and yet
i've never felt wealthier.
every penny that i spend gets replaced by
a crisp one hundred dollar bill
—the kind of bill that the cashier holds up to the light and
squints at.

this love isn't counterfeit or a knock off brand.
i always get more than i pay for with you.

shucking.

we shuck corn on the porch
as we prepare to make another dinner together.
a song is playing on the radio coated with static,
but you and i can still make out the words.
corn silk is blowing all over
as a thunderstorm begins to roll in.

"think we'll lose power?" you ask as you toss another
ear into the bucket.

"well, if we do, it'll be a version of a nitty gritty dirt band
song,"
i reply.

you raise your eyebrows and ask, "how so?"
i pick up the bucket of corn and head into the house
singing, "you and me eating dinner in the dark…"

sharpie on boxes.

we've been living out of cardboard boxes
and fast food containers.
styrofoam stacks fill our fridge and we have to
smell them to make sure they are still good enough to eat.
we haven't planted our roots yet.
we haven't found our forever home.
the coffee in our cups doesn't have a chance
to grow cold before we are onto our next location.
it won't be like this forever.
we'll find our place eventually.

"i just want to spend more than one christmas in a place,"
you say to me.

i don't know when that will be,
but i pull you in close to me and say, "soon."

soon you'll wake up in the same bed.
soon you'll have a favorite spot in the house to read.
soon you'll find a perfect place to put that christmas tree.

soon.

no agenda.

saturdays with you and no plans are dangerous.

we could be homebodies

or blow our paycheck on a day trip.

i never know where we'll end up.

there's something beautiful about that chaos.

morning discoveries.

a note from her on the coffee table
means more to me than any text message.

car troubles.

to see you with someone else breaks me.
the engine that i've been running on
begins to malfunction.
the gasoline ignites and burns my throat
as the motor attempts to carry on.
initially it hurts, but then i
just become numb to it all.

i ignore the check engine light.
the squeak of the brakes,
the oil changes,
the trembling hands,
the regret filled texts,
the blurry vision,
the stagger.

i often find myself at 2a.m. leaned up against my bedside
sitting and wondering why
my windshield wipers won't work.

one thousand apologies.

for all of the things i left unsaid,
please forgive me.

for all of the times i didn't make the bed,
please forgive me.

for all of the times that i was late
and all of the times i showed up way too early,
please forgive me.

for all of the times i should've kissed you, but didn't.
for all of the times i should've reached out for your hand,
but i kept it tucked into my pocket.
for all of the hugs that never came to be
and all of the venting sessions that never took place.

i can tell you i'm sorry all that i want,
but that still won't make up for my mistakes.

adding it all up.

it's simple addition.
it's adding up all of those little moments and creating one
"i love you."

sure, you have to do some subtracting
when the arguments come about.
but you can always bounce back with
a little multiplication on those big days.
the days when all you see is them.
no imaginary shopping lists pop into your head.
no errands that still need to be run.
no message that needs replying to.
it's you doing all that math in your head
concluding that you can't imagine life
without this person in it.

you only have to crunch the numbers once.
you know this is right where you're meant to be.

"not-so" smooth criminal.

i find your hairs on my sweatshirts
and it's such a beautiful discovery.
it doesn't take magnificent detectives
like sherlock holmes or the hardy boys
to solve these mini mysteries you leave for me.
the steam notes you leave for me
on the mirror while i am in the shower.
the pepperonis picked off of the pizza
and placed into a pile on a small paper plate.
the goofy faced selfies left on my phone
and set as my new wallpaper and background.

you leave traces of you everywhere
as if you want me to find you.

farmer's market.

we spend saturday mornings
knocking on watermelons,
smelling sweet corn,
flowers and trying free samples of honey.

"you could never pull off a fedora," you tell me.
"i could try," i say. "please don't," you reply.
before i can make a case for myself,
you're already shoveling salsa into my mouth.

we sleep in like we usually do on these saturday mornings.
there's no rush when you know the delicious harvests
will still be waiting for your senses to sample
well after ten o'clock.

we fill our bag full with these homegrown goodies
like two kids on halloween
that know where all the king size candy bars
are handed out at.

we aren't master chefs by any means,
but it's the days spent at the market
and the nights cooking in the kitchen
that take our taste buds on different adventures.

we don't need a passport or a tank full of gas,
just a good ear for melons,
some bargaining skills,
and a lazy saturday morning.

i don't mind.

i don't mind fixing the sink
or building something you found on pinterest.
it's how i show you that i love you.

i don't mind the miles that cause my odometer to spin as
we make our way to the north shore for the weekend.
the breeze catches your hand and hair
as you roll the windows down.
the sun finds your face and your shades hold on for dear
life like they would go to oakley purgatory
if they ever fell off.

"turn it up," you try to yell to me over the wind.

i crank the knob up, hoping that today won't be the day
i finally lose my hearing.
i still have yet to hear your voice say so many
  "i love you's".
i don't mind the long nights that find us on the weekends.
the mirror is unforgiving in the morning,
but i have never worried about being
the fairest of them all.

i brush my teeth as you sing in the shower,
but i have to spit out my toothpaste in laughter as you try
to rap the lines of shaggy's "it wasn't me."

i don't mind running the baths.
i don't mind going to the coffee shop concerts to support
your friends.
i don't mind your hair in my face in the morning.
i don't mind many things,
but i will let you know when i do
because that's how i show you that
i love you.

my imaginary loss.

it's crazy how the relationships that never happen are sometimes the ones we mourn the most.

hesitant hometown kid.

she's not the flavor of the week.
she's got that "bring her home to meet the parents"
way about her.
he wants to show her all the spots he used to go.
he longs to play tour guide in his hometown.
he feels obligated to give her the keys to the city,
but something holds him back.

something tells him not to show her every single spot.
he has to at least keep one special spot in his back pocket.
he doesn't want to think about it all going to hell,
but he has to at least acknowledge these thoughts.
if it all happens to blow up in his face,
this is where he'll have to retreat to fall in love
with his hometown all over again.

hold my hand.

"i'm not sure i can do this,"
you said as you examined the roller coaster.

your arms were crossed,
and you tilted your head back
so that you could see the tippy top.

"has anyone ever died on this thing?" you asked.
"yeah, just last week," i replied.

"what?" you said, "really?"
you tugged on my sweatshirt sleeve,
practically tearing it off of my shoulder.

"no," i said. "not really."

you lightly pushed me away
as i gave you a wide grin.

"don't say that kind of stuff, you goof," you said.
i pulled you in close to me and hugged you.
you hesitated a little,
but then i could feel you hug me back.

"you've got this," i said to you.

truth be told, if you didn't want to go on
i wouldn't have hesitated to walk out of that line with you,
grab a funnel cake,
and then make our way over to the merry-go-round.
but that's not your style.

"i can do this," you said.
you gave yourself a little pep talk
before we sat down in our seats.

you make me proud.
you squeezed my hand tightly during that ride,
but i don't mind losing the circulation
because sometimes it's me that's squeezing yours.

drive.

we shovel gas station snacks into our mouths.
the sugar finding our bloodstream
almost as quickly as a terrible hider
in a game of hide-and-seek.
we've got to try to stay awake.

"if i could hold open your eyelids while you drive
i would," you tell me,
which sounds a lot like "i love you" to me.
you crack open a red bull and hand it to me with a wink
only after you take a gulp first.

"how many miles do we have left?"
i ask while stretching my arms out.

"too many," you reply.
the miles we travel together may be hard on our bodies
with many pit stops along the way.
i will never forget the close call we had in tennessee
when you had to run in to use the bathroom.

"just drop me off and let me run in.
i'll tuck and roll if i have to,"
you said as you squeezed your legs together.
i don't think the car ever came to a complete stop.

with you it never does.

our little library in the woods.

she wants a house out in the country
with a wrap-around porch.
a little secluded, but easy enough to find
when she invites friends over for dinner.
she'll spend summer nights accompanied by
a glass of wine and a good book.
she'll have to hold down the pages
as the breeze tries to capture them speed her up.
she'll spend the winter months wrapped in a blanket
next to the fireplace
as she works her way down her reading list.

i'll work my fingers to the bone to give her this.
she'll look on from the porch as i split the wood
and stack it next to the house.
i'll ask her for updates on her story as i take little breathers.

"are you actually going to read this one," she asks me.

"yeah, eventually," i say
as I wipe the sweat from my face with my t-shirt.

i do get around to reading the books because
i like discussing them with her.
we talk about what characters are parallel to our friends
and what plot twists we saw coming.

i want to give her a place to call home.
a place to build her own library
where she doesn't have to worry about
return dates and packing them up into cardboard boxes.
a place to build her collection and our family.
our life will be a page turner
at our little library in the woods.

daze off.

she makes a little room for me
next to her on the pontoon.
the seats of the boat are sun faded
and are starting to show their age.
i lay my t-shirt onto the seat
and plop down next to her.

she's already working on her second white claw,
her sunglasses are slightly tilted off to the side.
the sunshine that finds her face leaves her
in a state of pure bliss
as she can't seem to stop smiling at me.

"we're never coming off the lake,"
she tells me as if i should start rationing
what food we have left on the boat.

two cans of pringles and tub of watermelon.
(yeah, we wouldn't make it too long.)

she needed this.
we needed this.
the lake is our therapy when we need
to step away from reality for a while.
it's our solace.
our happy place
—until a family swings by a little too close while tubing
and rocks our boat.
she spills her drink onto the front of her swimsuit.
she cleans up what little mess she made of herself.

"freakin' tourists."

frequent flyer.

the goodbyes never seem to get any easier
even if you're only gone for a week.
i feel like i am waiting forever in line at the grocery store
because there's a coupon wizard in front of me.
i know you'll find your way back to me.

you always do.

but that doesn't make the waiting game any easier on me.
i occupy my time with movies i have been meaning to
watch and that book you left on the counter.
i promise i won't spark notes this one.
you can probably tell right away when i do that anyways.

i take the dog on longer walks, hoping that when we make
our way back down the drive
you'll be sitting on the front porch with that
is-there-something-in-my-teeth wide smile.
i don't want to make you feel guilty for traveling.
that's not my intention at all.
i just want you to know that even though we may be many
miles apart, i filled your carry-on bag with love letters
written on postcards from home.

sleeping alone.

there are going to be nights that I end up
sleeping on the couch.
i don't plan on making it a habit.

let's keep the nights of going to bed angry
with one another to a minimum.
i know this is easier said than done.
seemingly little things turn into arguments
and our voices grow hoarse over a set of towels
that have yet to be folded.

to say that we won't have disagreements
is about as unrealistic
as you and I finding a flying magic carpet
and riding it over the city one night.
let's keep our love for one another
at the forefront of our arguments.
let's not turn out the lights when we are
fuming with anger
but find a way to figure it out.

figure us out.

waco.

"take me to the silos," you said as we watched another episode of *fixer upper*.

you must have been expecting an answer of "eventually," from me because when i said, "let's go next week," you would have thought i told your eight-year-old self that we were going to disney world.

we packed up the jeep and embarked on a road trip to the place where they say everything is bigger.
we both had never been to texas, but the fear of an adventure never held us back before.
by the third stop to go to the bathroom, get gas and grab a quick bite to eat, we were already sick of fast food.
we bought loaves of bread and peanut butter and jelly.
some may call us cheapskates.
we call ourselves,
"wise investors."

we stopped along the way to take pictures next to signs that caught our eyes and that only we would laugh about later.

we finally made it to waco and you could no longer
contain your excitement.
sure, you were sleeping the last three hours of the trip, but
when i poked you awake
telling you we were only ten miles way,
i should've mentally prepared more for your scream.

i love what you've done with our home and know you'll
make a great mother one day.
our home is important to me
and so is keeping the woman living in it happy.
so when you said, "take me to the silos,"
how could i turn you down?

out on the pier.

"let's stop here," you say as you plop down on the bench.

we've been walking for a while now
the neon lights seem to guide our path back to our car.
the boardwalk belongs only to us
 and a few stray seagulls picking at treasures tucked in
between the sun faded boards.

"you thinking what i'm thinking?" you say as you raise
your eyebrows and flash a smile.
you direct your gaze over to the sign that says, *Ruby's*.

"definitely," i reply, "i'll be right back."
we're past the point of me needing to ask you
what you want to eat.
you've stolen fries from my plate enough
for me to know that by now.
you still try to sneak them into your mouth by taking them
when i appear to be looking away,
but you make a terrible thief.
i also like how we're past the point of always
feeling the need to have constant dialogue.

i used to think silence made things awkward
or that our connection was lost.
but there are moments that find us like a heads up penny
on the ground and the moment speaks for itself.

plus one.

it's been harder to go to weddings.
i'm not saying that i'm not happy for the married couple,
but they continue to serve as a constant reminder of
how lonely i am without you.

i make small talk at my singles table.
(it wasn't that hard to figure out)
i talk about my job,
but what i really want to be doing is bragging about you.
i know you always hated the spotlight being on us.

i miss my dancing partner.
we may not have been baby and johnny,
but we held our own.
towards the end of the night,
we always seemed to be the last ones out on the floor.

i miss having you as my plus one.
but you've been gone for a while now
and you're probably catching bouquets
with someone else in mind.

thunderstorm therapy.

we spent all weekend cooped up in the house.
the thunderstorms rattled and shook
our tiny apartment on davis street.
the neighbor's dog yipped along with the booms
like it was trying to keep rhythm
with mother nature's angry symphony.

the lights flickered every now and then,
turning our living room into a brief night club.
we were eating delivery pizza while clinging to the fading
battery life of my laptop as we watched
the lowest rated movies on netflix.

throughout this summer we haven't even been able to fix
the broken watch on our wrists that we keep checking.
between college friends' weddings on the weekends
to taking on extra shifts at work, our lives seem to be a
flicker rather than a slow burn.
this thunderstorm therapy we experience
is the tap on the roof
and the tap on the shoulder we needed.

more sugar, please.

"just let me cook, you said.
but it's never that simple with you and me.

there must be a mess to clean up.
there must be a stack of dishes in the sink.
the bubbles build upon one another
and stretch themselves as if they are making a feeble
attempt at touching the ceiling fan.

i wish we could cook together every night.
our grocery lists would be longer.
our shopping carts would give off the impression that we
are wealthier than the generic boxes of cereal that poke
themselves out from behind the milk cartons.
we'd still carry all of the bags into the house in one trip
though.

we aren't rookies.

various big band music would radiate from our speakers
whether we were cooking a fancy italian meal
or just some french toast.

it's much more than cooking.
more than the simple consumption of food.
it goes beyond the swishing of our drinks in our mouths
and the chewing of the various meals.
it's the time spent together.

as we brush off the scraps from our days
we put in spoonfuls of the sugar
we were waiting all day to touch our tongues.

a few requests.

may flowers find the vase on the kitchen table
more often than not.
may kisses find your cheek in the front seat of cars,
photo booths, after a good day or bad day at work,
and at the gas station just because you're my girl.

may blankets conceal a cheap bottle of wine
as we make our way up the hillside
to get a better view of the stars.

may the car need oil changes more often
from the miles we travel together.

may the change jar above the fridge treat us
to rainy day adventures
that leave our clothes soaking wet
and cause our dryer to work overtime.

may the prayers we say along with dinner get answered
and if they don't,
may our faith refuse to waver.

may we be intentional with one another

and when we argue,

may we put away our pride and work things out together.

you make great company.

i think i want to keep you around.

wishful thinking.

i wish i met you earlier.
i wish i met you when you were still in high school and your biggest worry was that chemistry final and who was going to ask you to the homecoming dance.

i wish i met you earlier when you still had a curfew to mind and your father still cleaned that gun at the kitchen table.

i wish i met you when you worked at that tiny grocery store on the corner and the elderly men would pay you compliments every time they went through your lane.

i wish i met you before that drive-in theater played its final film and all of those trees found the lumber yard.

i wish i met you earlier, but i'm glad i met you now.

throwing out my racing bib.

i love slow mornings and slow evenings with you.
it allows me to take deep breaths
when life begins to feel like a sprint.

sometimes i feel like i'm the slowest runner in this race.
i haven't trained enough.
i'm sweating and breathing heavily,
not really sure if i will ever reach that finish line.

"you're thinking too much again, babe," you say as you
turn over and look at me.

i take my eyes off of the ceiling, not really sure
how long i've gone without blinking.
i look at you and all of the worries scatter
like kids on a playground playing tag.

"we'll figure things out together," you tell me, "but for
now, let's listen to the songs of the morning."

i twist over the window locks and slide the window open,
exposing the dew coated screen.

we both take a tremendous whiff of the fresh rain
and break into laughter.

"it smells like we're going to live forever. like nothing
could get better than this."

i forget about the race.
i forget about the time.
i forget about pleasing other people.

all i can smell is the rain, hear the birds, and feel your
presence.

long drives & short nights together.

our summer jobs kept us from seeing each other
for weeks on end.
phone calls drained our phone batteries.
crinkled letters found our mailboxes.
they got us by until we could see each other.
we'd only get a couple of days together,
but we crammed our summer within those weekends.

we couldn't take many road trips,
but you rode shotgun blindfolded,
telling me when to turn and when to stop.
we caught movies in the middle of the day
so we could spend our nights out on the town.

i didn't mind those nights when we decided to stay in.
we talked about what life would look like outside
of this rearview mirror town
and where we wanted to settle down.
we wish our summer nights would be infinite,
but there are student loans to pay off
and rent payments to make
that always seem to come too soon.

facetime.

our faces found the kiss cam.
they didn't know it was our first date.
i didn't even know
how many siblings you had.
i didn't know what your hardest laugh sounded like.

they didn't know that i haven't seen your
we-need-to-pet-that-stranger's-dog face
without you ever saying a word.

they didn't know that i haven't seen you
when you're sick.

they didn't know that i haven't seen you
when you're hangry.

they didn't know that i haven't stopped by your work yet
to drop off lunch when you forgot yours at home.

they didn't know,
but that didn't stop you
from planting your lips on mine.

loud mouth.

i love bragging about you.
i love showing you off.
i see you with clear eyes.
you're beautiful, but that doesn't do you enough justice.
it's not in a conventional way.

you're beautiful like a watercolor painted sky in the middle
of summer at the top of a ferris wheel.
you're beautiful like a movie that makes me laugh,
nervously shake, and cry all at the same time.
you're beautiful like rain tapping on the roof
as we've got an afternoon of no plans
and a fully stocked fridge.

i love bragging about how smart you are.
you rattle off names of these characters from
the novels that fill your milk crate bookshelves
and leave me in awe.

i love that you're active in the community.
i don't think i've had an open weekend since we met,
but i don't mind.
this stuff is going to look killer on my resume if i ever
decide to switch jobs.

(come on, i'm only joking.)

so yes, i love bragging about you because it amazes me that
not everybody sees you the way i do.

magic.

she brings magic into my life
like it's my first time reading harry potter all over again.

a little box in my pocket.

all of my life i've waited for this moment.
standing before you now, i know this to be true.
i wish i could coach my body better.
knees—stop shaking.
heart—please, slow down your beat.
hands—steady yourselves.
but it's no use.
i tremble anyways as my knee finds the lush summer grass.

those four words seem so simple now.
i must have practiced in the mirror for hours on end.
i had to make sure my tone was right.
that my smile was that favorite one of yours.
i had to make sure my posture was correct.
i began to stress myself out.
the kind of stress that has me cleaning
out the cupboards and feeling ten pounds heavier.
then i realized that it's you and me.

it's simple.
this is what love should feel like.
looking into each other's eyes and knowing no matter what
everything is going to be okay.

ABOUT THE AUTHOR

Thank you for reading the ramblings of my heart. If you ever want to grab a cup of coffee or a brew, I am usually not that hard to find. I want to hear about the trips you want to take, the girl or guy you've been talking to and what sticks out to you about them, why you're thinking about leaving your job, what's on your bucket list, etc. Maybe you don't see us as that good of friends and if that's the case—I understand. I'll admit I'm a pretty shy guy. Those conversations aren't for everybody and why should you trust me to talk to? But if you ever need someone to talk to when the beer just isn't getting the job done, I'm an open ear. I'm just your friendly neighborhood hopeful romantic trying to figure this life out one notebook page at a time.

-Dalton Hessel